Cruising
for
Seniors

Cruising
for
Seniors

Paul H. Keller

With contributions by
Mark R. Anderson, MD, Emily Tufts Keller,
Harry Mitchell and John Strong

S

Sheridan House

First published 2000 by
Sheridan House Inc.
145 Palisade Street
Dobbs Ferry, NY 10522

Library of Congress Cataloging-in-Publication Data

Keller, Paul H.
    Cruising for seniors / Paul H. Keller ; assisted by Mark R. Anderson,
Emily Tufts Keller, Harry Mitchell and John Strong.
        p. cm.
    Includes bibliographical references.
    ISBN 1-57409-086-0 (alk. paper)
    1. Boats and boating. 2. Aged—Recreation. I. Anderson, Mark R.,
M.D. II. Keller, Emily Tufts. III. Mitchell, Harry. IV. Strong, John.
V. Title.

GV775.K35 2000
797.1'24'0846—dc21   00-058827

Edited by Catherine Degnon
Designed by Kirby J. Kiskadden

Printed in the United States of America

Old age has yet his honour and his toil;
Death closes all: but something ere the end,
Some work of noble note, may yet be done,
Not unbecoming men that strove with Gods.
The lights begin to twinkle from the rocks;
The long day wanes: the slow moon climbs: the deep
Moans round with many voices. Come, my friends,
'Tis not too late to seek a newer world.
Push off, and sitting well in order smite
The sounding furrows; for my purpose holds
To sail beyond the sunset, and the baths
Of all the western stars, until I die.
It may be that the gulfs will wash us down:
It may be we shall touch the Happy Isles,
And see the great Achilles, whom we knew.
Though much is taken, much abides; and though
We are not now that strength which in old days
Moved earth and heaven; that which we are, we are;
One equal temper of heroic hearts,
Made weak by time and fate, but strong in will
To strive, to seek, to find, and not to yield.

Alfred, Lord Tennyson, from "Ulysses"

CONTENTS

PREFACE

After I wrote my first book, *Sailing the Golden Sea*, my wife, Emily, and I devoted a lot of time to its promotion, which included numerous appearances at retirement homes. Many of the people there who talked with us after our slide presentations expressed amazement that I was in my sixties and Emily nearly so when we first started our globe-circling. Once, at the conclusion of my remarks, a man audibly sighed, "And here we sit."

This gentleman struck me as one of those many retirees who had once dreamed the dream but thought they were too old now even to contemplate such an adventure. As I thought about his remark, I recalled the many retired people we had met while cruising and the many who had had gray hair; we were not that unique. The number of people over the age of fifty-five is growing rapidly, and as a group, these seniors are both healthier and more prosperous than their predecessors were. Many with a great number of "golden years" still to come will have once had dreams of sailing some day. But how many will ever find this dream realized?

It seems to me that mental attitude is the primary deterrent for most would-be cruisers. Some fear physical infirmities, but for most, perhaps the greatest fear of all is fear of the unknown. This book is designed to address most of the issues that keep so many retirees from sailing off into the sunset. If you are one such dreamer, maybe this book will help you overcome your fears and find the courage to tell your friends on the dock, "Okay, cast off our lines. Here we go to a new life!"

Obviously, such a book requires expertise that is beyond my scope. For me, casting off the lines was easy—I have been an adventurer all my life. I have had the help of others. For many potential cruisers, the primary issue revolves around age: "I am over sixty; I am approaching that time of life when people develop new age-related problems. How will I recognize and cope at sea or in some remote primitive place?" While Emily is a doctor, her specialty, pediatrics, is at the wrong end of the age spectrum, so to discuss that issue, I called on Dr. Mark Anderson. His chapter addresses these geriatric considerations as completely as possible. Dr. Anderson is also a sailor who is building a magnificent cruising boat, plank by plank, in a shed in his backyard.

Harry Mitchell was very helpful with a chapter on the weather. Next, I needed someone to give me a complete and up-to-date analysis of electric and electronic considerations. John Strong, a marine surveyor who knows as much about everything in a sailboat as any man I have ever known, readily agreed to write this chapter. I was more than delighted; his firm had overhauled the electrics on SUNSET, our current boat, and we are more than satisfied with the results.

Nadine Cobb presented my idea for a book to Lothar Simon of Sheridan House. Their endorsements are why this book exists. It also existed for a while as an idea that Sharon Castlen encouraged me to develop and submit. My wife, Emily,

Preface

not only encouraged me but also agreed to write a chapter on women's concerns. I also appealed to my many cruising friends for suggestions and owe much to Larry Davis, Jim Henshaw, Clyde Coffee, Jay Davis, and others. And while many of the suggestions in this book come from my own experience, many more came from conversations all over the world with commodores of the Seven Seas Cruising Association and other cruisers.

Rereading the chapters of this book, I notice that I use a lot of nautical terminology to describe various equipment and techniques, which some would-be adventurers with little sailing experience may find daunting. This salty talk is necessary, and to explain every term would double the size of the book. If you are new to sailing and boats, I trust you to refer to the references in the appendix. I'll just explain one term—the bow is the pointy end.

Paul H. Keller

INTRODUCTION

I met Emily on the ski slopes of Mount Hood in Oregon. I was teaching business and economics on a part-time basis at several colleges in the Portland area after retiring from Warner Pacific College and was a ski instructor on weekends. I had a cruising boat of offshore caliber and was preparing to leave the following fall on a round-the-world cruise. Emily, who was teaching pediatrics at Oregon Health Sciences University in Portland, wanted to upgrade her skiing skills with a one-hour private lesson. The ski school chose me as her instructor. That was the beginning of a relationship that developed into marriage and ten years of living on a boat, cruising the world.

Because of my self-imposed schedule, I left the following September. Our engagement was public, and the plan was to be married by a holy man of whatever faith was available when Emily joined me the following July someplace in the South Pacific (she needed time to retire properly from her position). How romantic, I thought. Emily had some misgivings but agreed. However, when I called her from San Diego in November, I was persuaded to fly back to get married in Portland. I returned bearing a couple of gold rings. Emily's friends, the Buist family, had a wonderful wedding planned, and it was skillfully executed. Now, I thought, she can't change her mind while I'm off sailing around the world. Now, she thought, those beautiful Polynesian women are no longer a threat.

In June, Emily put her former life and furniture in storage. On June 30 she was on call at the hospital. On July 1 she boarded a plane for Tahiti and a life such as she had never known. Not that her life had not been adventurous. After graduating from medical school, she opened a small-town practice in Pinehurst, North Carolina. Ten years later she accepted a teaching position in Portland, on the other side of the continent. Her appetite for adventure was met by the great mountains, valleys, and forests of the Pacific Northwest. She sought new experiences occasionally with painting trips to France, hiking in the Alps, and a trek to Mount Everest base camp. Her job became stressful when she was assigned to the abused child program. Apparently I happened into her life at just the right time.

With a fine appreciation for the opposite sex, I had been looking for the right companion to serve as first mate. Born in Nebraska, which is about as far from the sea as you can get, I had played with boats as a child and read sea stories voraciously. I attribute this early attraction to an unconfirmed but often-admired and -imitated pirate ancestor. My fascination with the sea was strengthened by a stint in the navy during World War II. My mature years were spent raising and providing for a family. I never lost my desire to set to sea, though, and when the nest was empty, I sought to realize it. My wife would have no part of such apparent foolishness, and as often happens when a born sailor is faced with the choice of a boat or a settled lifestyle, the latter loses. Finally I reached a time in my life when it seemed possible to realize my dream, and for ten years I worked toward it.

Everything fell into place when I met Emily. The rest of the story is told in my previous two books, *Sailing the Golden Sea* and *Sailing the Inland Seas*. The first chronicles our adventures in the South Pacific and Europe. The second describes our two-year journey up the Intracoastal Waterway of the East Coast, through the Erie Canal and Great Lakes, down the great rivers and canals of America's heartland, and back to Florida. The voyages started in Portland, Oregon, and ended ten years later in Florida. I was sixty-four and Emily was fifty-nine when we left for the South Pacific. Our only home for those ten years was our boat (we had three during this period). We had a condominium for the final two years, but used it only occasionally as a home base when we returned to Portland for visits. Now, fully retired from our life as sea vagabonds, we still have a boat and spend summers cruising the vast protected areas of the Pacific Northwest's fjords and island archipelagoes. Oh yes, we still ski.

1

To Go or Not to Go

First, let me tell you what this book is about and what it isn't. It provides answers to the many questions that people no longer in their youth have when they dream of setting sail on an extended voyage. It is not a complete how-to guide. If you want to learn sail design, rigging, boat building, engine maintenance, navigation, performance sailing, first-aid afloat, weather prediction, and other skills that you might need while voyaging, start by looking to the references discussed in the appendix. This book addresses only the sailing basics necessary to the dreamers and the romantics. If you meet those two qualifications, then read on.

Lives there a man or woman who has stood on a cliff high above the sea gazing to the far horizon and not longed to sail off into the sunset? Lives there a man who has read of the adventures of Jack London, Sir Francis Chichester, Eric and Susan Hiscock, Larry and Lin Pardey, and a host of other voyagers, and not sighed and said, "I'd like to do that myself some day"?

Before I left for the South Pacific, such dreams filled my mind every time I went to the shore or strolled on the beach. I suppose that the difference between those who go and those who stay is some primitive drive that exists in our genes; certainly there was never a doubt in my mind that someday I would go to sea. I hope that somewhere in this book you, too, will find the determination to go.

Yet there are so many questions and so few ready answers. So that you may not be among those who dream these dreams but turn away with a sigh, here are many of the questions seniors ask and some responses based on Emily's and my experience and that of many other cruisers.

Q. At fifty-five (or sixty-five or seventy), am I not too old for this foolishness?

A. When I recall the many cruisers we met during our ten years in this lifestyle, it seems that more than half had gray hair. Once, when we were in England, a sailboat ending a three-day passage from Gibraltar docked just behind us. A slim, gray-haired woman jumped down on the dock, quickly flipped a bowline knot into the line she held and looped it over a cleat, returned to the boat, and did the same with the stern line. "Nicely done," I said. She answered, "Should be, I've been doing it for twenty years. However, my husband and I are slowing down, and we may have to pack it in in a few more years. I'm eighty, and he's eighty-one."

My point is that medical science has extended our life span and for most of us also enriched it with good health. Old is more a mental condition than a physical one. Of course, "We are not now that strength which in old days moved earth and heaven" (Tennyson, in "Ulysses"), but there are many ways to compensate for this reduced strength. Helping you find them is one of the purposes of this book.

There are two basic categories of cruisers: part-timers and

liveaboards. Part-timers, for various reasons, maintain their home and connections ashore but cruise for periods of several weeks or months. They are akin to the "snow birds" from the northern states and Canada who populate the South during the winter months. On the East Coast, the Intracoastal Waterway is choked each fall and spring with cruisers moving their boats south for the winter and north for the summer. Others simply keep their boats in southern waters as a sort of winter vacation home. Some part-timers cruise Europe or Asia during the summer and return home to work for the winter months (or vice versa), leaving their boat on the hard, or hauled out, for several months. The point is that these people enjoy their boats as much as liveaboards, but the boat is never their *real* home.

SUNSET, our boat, lies at anchor in the Pacific Northwest.

Liveaboards free themselves from the ties that bind them to the land, move aboard their watery home, and roam the seas, sometimes with only vague agendas. When you ask them where they are going, they answer something like this: "We'll spend perhaps a couple of years in the Caribbean and then maybe transit through the canal to the South Pacific, and then, who knows?" We have several West Coast friends who never got any farther than New Zealand, where they spent several years (some are still there). They live inexpensively, and some even take employment doing something that they always wanted to do. One of our friends became a scuba instructor, another became a welder, and many work in boatyards. One woman took along her Moog synthesizer and composed for CDs that she sold.

When you have this kind of freedom you have joined an exclusive community of people who are living their lives to the fullest—world cruisers. Of course, it is not a geriatric community by any means. Many in it are young couples who sail awhile and then find local employment of any kind to replenish their cruising kitty. While we were in Turkey, Emily was not feeling well, and since we had plans to meet a friend who had just gone through the Red Sea, we hired a very fine sailor to accompany us to Cyprus. The young skipper's wife was seven months pregnant but wanted to go along. We still hear from them; they are still living aboard, and their son now has a baby sister.

If this latter lifestyle is the vision in your dreams, I suggest that you bite the bullet and sell your home and any other real estate. "What! Sell the family home that has so many memories? What will we do with our furniture? What if the kids want to come and visit us? How about our friends, neighbors, grandchildren?" If all these factors are more important to you than your dream or desire for adventure, you are not ready to go. But ponder this: I think that my children admire us for what we did more than they would have if we had stayed home and maintained a spare bedroom for them to visit. We returned home once a year at Christmas and celebrated with family and friends. The freedom that you have when you leave unencumbered is so different from what you experience if you leave with responsibilities. If this comment sounds a little irresponsible, isn't that what retirement is all about?

Q. Speaking of responsibilities, how much does it cost to go cruising?

A. I think it was Lin or Larry Pardey who, when asked, "How much?" replied, "As much as you have." This is a good answer depending on how tight your budget is. I once asked a couple who planned to spend the next two years in the South Pacific and then return to Portland, "How much will you need to do this?"

"We have four thousand saved up in our cruising kitty," they responded.

"For crying out loud!" I gasped. "You can't live for two years on four thousand dollars. No way."

"Our budget has been carefully made out, including dinner ashore once a month and an annual haul-out for bottom painting. Remember, we own our boat free and clear; we have been fitting her out for the last two years; and we're vegetarians and have several sacks of the basic foods aboard. We will make it and be back here in two years broke but with wonderful memories. Life can't get any better than that."

I had to agree.

But what about everyone else? Most retirees have a comfortable income. Either way, you have lifestyle choices. You can stay in first-class marinas or anchor out. You can rent cars to visit inland sights or take the bus—or walk, even! You can spend a lot of money on your boat buying new gadgets. You can eat out frequently and buy gifts for friends and relatives. You can also hire local people to fix, paint, and overhaul your boat. Or you can plan on self-sufficiency, like the young couple above (the necessary skills to do so are discussed in later chapters).

Q. What about health care and first aid?

A. First, if you are generally in poor health, don't go. But if you are in good health or have a manageable problem, you have no reason not to go. Chapter 10 addresses this question in detail, focusing on those emergencies that are specific to or have a higher frequency of occurrence among seniors, but here are some basic answers. Every country in the world offers medical services. Evacuation services are available almost everywhere. There are a number of books on first aid and emergencies at sea. In short, if you are in good health, go. If you worry a lot about your health, don't go.

The most ludicrous fear I have had expressed to me came from an individual who, at a party, asked if I still had my appendix. I answered, "Yes, why?"

"Well, surely you are going to have it out before you go, aren't you?"

"Of course not. Why should I?"

"Obviously you've never had appendicitis. What if you have it in the middle of the ocean?"

"I'm sixty-three years old," I replied. "Since I have not had it yet, I think my odds of escaping it during my lifetime are pretty good. Besides, I take good care of my body, and that is all any one can do."

If you see yourself in my questioner, don't go.

Q. What if you have an accident?

A. If you feel that you have no control over your actions or if you feel you might not have enough ingenuity to extricate yourself from difficult situations, your cruising life will be one of terror over what might happen, instead of pleasure from what did happen. The kinds of accidents that could happen are covered in the chapter on safety. The text focuses particularly on the prevention of accidents that have happened to others and to me. Accident prevention includes preparing the boat for safety and having ironclad rules regarding your own actions and those of your crew. Safety harnesses are a good example. We had one unbreakable rule on our boats: At sea we never went on deck without snapping on our safety harness. When one of us in a moment of panic or excitement failed to observe the rule, the other would berate the perpetrator none too gently. It was loving criticism.

Q. It must be pretty boring at sea. What do you do: Read a lot? Or fish?

A. This question expresses one of the common misconceptions about ocean sailing. First, you spend very little time actually at sea compared with the amount of time you spend in harbors and ashore visiting and sightseeing. You may make a three-day passage to the next island and then spend three months there at anchor.

Second, there is much to see and do at sea. Wildlife is

abundant. Flying fish and squid littered our decks daily. Tuna paced us in the ship's shadow. Whales, dolphins, and seabirds swirl and whirl around the boat. Once a great big shark followed us for an hour. Pelagic birds visit for a while to satisfy their curiosity. Fishing, however, is not a pastime on a passage. While you can trail a line and bring in a tuna or mahi-mahi, catching such fish is only exciting if you love to eat fish. Fishing can quickly translate into hard work and too much fish.

Finally, you have to run the boat, which involves at a minimum sail changing, navigation, checking the compass, taking sights, and reading charts. And of course, someone has to be on watch at all times, even in mid-ocean, to keep a lookout for other boats, especially freighters.

In addition, there are always naps during the day to compensate for watches stood at night, meals to prepare, and laundry and personal hygiene to attend to. Yes, you do read some, but aboard our boats, there didn't seem to be much time for it—especially since we spent a lot of time staring at the ocean. If that seems a little silly, have you ever sat around a campfire at night?

Q. What about currency, immigration, language, and shots?

A. These issues all need to be dealt with, but the problems are always solvable. Dealing with the last issue first, I never got any shots. Neither did Emily—and she is a doctor. In years past immunization shots were important because many diseases only infrequently encountered here in the United States or Canada were common elsewhere in the world. With international travel now so inexpensive and frequent, those differences have pretty much disappeared, however. Discuss your concerns with your own doctor, of course.

12

To Go or Not To Go

Immigration and customs present a different kind of problem. There are countries that we would not visit, for the most part because their governments were hostile; some of the Red Sea countries are examples. However, in all our travels we have yet to receive other than a friendly reception. We encountered a few individual customs agents who felt that exerting their authority was more important than making tourists feel welcome, but in those kinds of situations, patience and respect always win. Argument and confrontation seldom do. Sometimes a five-dollar bill in your hand, neatly folded but visible, smooths your way, although in almost every country bribery is illegal. Sometimes, though, local offices charge a "processing fee." A

When we entered a lock in the French canals, Emily first had to climb a slimy ladder carrying two heavy rope loops which she dropped on the bollards. She then walked back and assisted the éclusier (lock keeper) by closing the gate on her side. She practiced her French on the éclusier.

case in point: As we were leaving the Cook Islands for Tonga we talked on the ham radio with a couple we had met in an earlier anchorage. One particular customs officer, they said, always asked if there was liquor aboard and then proceeded to sample it for an hour or so while he "made you feel welcome" in Tonga. Our friend advised us to say that we had none aboard.

On the subject of language, all I can say is that we never found it a problem. Remember that the purpose of language is to communicate and that words are only one way to do so. We have drawn pictures and used sign language and phrase books. These substitutes worked pretty well, but we seldom needed to resort to them since almost everywhere in the world someone speaks a little English and is eager to use it. Besides, all of our attempts to communicate in foreign languages were received with good humor and not a little merriment—except in Paris. (Ah well! Paris is Paris.)

Currency? We never had any serious problems getting local currency. Any bank will advance you local currency on your credit cards. American dollars (and other hard currencies) are another matter. Once, we needed US $1,000 to pay off a fisherman who had towed our boat into the Greek island of Kárpathos. We telephoned our bank and asked that they wire that amount to the local bank. Two days later we were informed the money had arrived. At the bank, I waited patiently to retrieve the dollars while the manager was busy with his calculator. Finally I asked what he was doing. "Computing the amount in drachmas," he answered. I said I didn't want drachmas; the money was to be delivered in dollars. "But I don't have any dollars," he said.

"Yes, you do," I replied. "My bank just wired you one thousand of them. They are mine, and I'd like them." After consulting with his superior in Athens, he went to the vault, and I got my dollars.

In short, money is not a problem, and you don't have to carry large sums with you. A few hundred dollars in traveler's checks and a good credit card are about all you need. In some places, Istanbul for instance, where there was strong inflation, you could get much more for U.S. dollars or any other strong currency. The taxi drivers much preferred dollars to the Turkish lira.

Q. Where will I ever acquire all the skills I'll need?

A. There are many sources, among them community colleges, power squadrons, the U.S. Coast Guard Auxiliary, and yacht clubs. Magazines and books devoted to sailing abound and are loaded with knowledge. Before you sell your house and buy a boat, you might charter one with a professional skipper and pump him or her for ideas and opinions (the sailing magazines *Cruising World* and *Sail* carry extensive charter advertisements). Or you could follow a method employed by many cruisers: Start with a small sailboat, move to a somewhat bigger one in a year or two, and then get your cruising boat. During that time join a yacht club. In two or three years you will be ready to go.

A friend, a former navy officer, when he learned of my writing this book, sent me a cautionary letter, the gist of which was, "Paul, please don't try to write a book that has people thinking that once they've read it, they're ready to take off and sail around the world." This, of course, is not my objective. I don't think you will buy a boat, cast off your lines, and sail out to sea without knowing a great deal about what you are doing. You should become one with your boat, so that you know what to do in almost every circumstance and are able to do it without thinking. When you naturally start calling the boat *she*, you are ready.

A singular characteristic of cruisers is that they are identified by first names and their boat names. We were Paul and Emily on GOLDEN FLEECE. There was Don and Rhoda on SUNCHASER, and Joan and David on PSYCHE, and many others. Remembering their last names did not seem very important.

Q. But my God! There we go out on the ocean with little experience in a small boat, and I don't have all the skills to handle all exigencies! That is asking for trouble!

A. Of course it is. Don't do that. Sail your boat until you feel that you are in charge. Get to know its peculiarities well. Our second cruiser, a Westsail 32, was very sluggish coming about so we gybed more often than we came about. We practiced this maneuver many times. How to heave-to is another technique that needs enough practice so that you can do it almost automatically. Remember, if you have the right boat for cruising, the weak link in emergencies is the skipper. I never (well, almost never) worried in a storm because I knew I had a strong boat that could survive it. What constitutes a strong boat is covered more fully in the next chapter.

In the early stages of your dream making you have to face reality. Do you think that you are just as capable as a good share of the sailors out there cruising the oceans? Do you believe that if they are cruising, you can be, too? If you do, then a great life of adventure awaits you.

There are two factors that may keep you ashore. The first is that curse known as *mal de mer*, or seasickness. Although I can't point to statistics, it is my belief that at least half of all cruisers are afflicted at one time or another. Some feel sick for the first day or two at sea; others are afflicted only when they have a cold or some other infection. Some are affected in storms. And so it goes. In fact, it seems that seniors are less affected and that age brings a diminution of seasickness. It has something to do with the inner ear being less sensitive. There are also many helpful remedies. To find out how you react to sea motion, I suggest a few trial cruises. Emily and I are blessed with freedom from this curse, but we have both been sick on occasion. Even if you do get seasick, there is no reason for you to stay ashore and curse your genes. As I tried to emphasize earlier, the time spent at sea is only a fraction of the time you devote to cruising. The greatest part is spent in port interacting with the local culture.

The other monumental problem you may face is that your spouse of many years may consider your scheme absolutely ridiculous. There are only two ways to solve this problem: Get another spouse or give up your dream. This assertion is brusque and blunt, but you must realize that any compromise is going to strain the relationship to the limits. If your spouse plans to join the boat at various spots around the globe, remember that there will be months you will be apart and that there are a lot of attractive people of the opposite sex out there who want to crew. At this time Emily and I have several friends, males and females, who are looking for either skipper or crew. I use the word spouse advisedly. We have also found that the thrill of adventure is not related in anyway to the gender of the individual. All over the world there are women looking for skippers and skippers looking for women. All love to sail and live the adventurous life. These are active, vital, living people, many of whom have just retired and are now living a lifelong dream. You can join them if you wish.

2

THE BOAT

Sir Francis Chichester, who circumnavigated the world in the 1960s when wooden boats were still dominant, said that he would never go to sea in a boat that displaced less than 7 tons. Then, tonnage was a good comparative measure of a boat's strength, because heavier timbers and stout planking implied stronger boats, given similar design and dimensions. Modern materials, because they are much stronger than wood, have made a boat's tonnage less of a criterion for seaworthy cruising. I tend to like the weight anyway, because greater weight makes a more sea-friendly boat.

Our present boat, SUNSET, is a Nauticat 38, a motorsailer, and displaces 12 tons. Our previous boat, a Westsail 32, displaced 7 tons. We commenced our cruising life in a Westsail 28 that displaced 6 tons. Westsails were among the top cruisers of their time (the company also offered a 42). They were built of fiberglass with a thick, heavy hull and heavy spars and standing rigging. The weak factor was the skipper—me. I never worried that the boat would break up in spite of some pretty fierce storms that assailed us. And when we got knocked down in the Atlantic on GOLDEN BELL, our Westsail 32, she righted beautifully.

19

Let me tell you of a different approach to displacement that we saw in the South Pacific. The boat's owner was a young lawyer who had settled a big case and decided to take two years off and sail around the world. He had budgeted his expenses carefully, including meals out, car rentals, and so on. He was sailing a 30-foot plywood boat that he said was the best boat that he could get for what he had left of the settlement. When I remarked on the lightness of its construction, he said he was not worried because he would outrun storms and get to safe harbors quickly. The sea is a demanding mistress and does not coddle fools. I often think of him and wonder if his luck ever ran out.

The different types of materials used in boat construction

GOLDEN BELL, our Westsail 32, hauled out in Alicante, Spain. Note the full keel and ample rudder: both are useful for good performance downwind. Since most cruisers prefer to go downwind, this is one of the favored hulls.

each has strengths and disadvantages, and there is certainly no consensus among cruisers as to which is best for long-distance voyaging. The same holds for the design and construction of the boat's other components: keel, cabin and decks, and interior. The point is to find the best match for *your* particular needs. For example, you want to look at the budget for not only the boat itself but also ongoing maintenance. And you want to be realistic in your expectations about both boat performance and your own physical performance. My best advice is to employ a naval architect to advise you and perhaps even design a boat for your needs. Alternatively, you could seek advice from a marine surveyor and then have him inspect any boat that you are considering purchasing.

Hull materials. Most of today's production boats are made of *fiberglass*, also called GRP (glass-reinforced plastic). It is probably true that you can get the most safety for your money from this material. The hull's thickness is the best indication of the boat's strength. Fiberglass hulls consist of multiple layers of glass fibers saturated with polyester resin. The more layers there are, the stronger the vessel. Ask if core samples of the hull are available when you are considering the purchase of a particular boat. Take them to your adviser and get an opinion. Again, in general, the heavier the displacement, the stronger the boat. Familiarize yourself with typical displacements for the length of boat you are considering. Also compute how much of the displacement is represented by ballast. Compare, for example, two boats whose displacements are 12,000 pounds; one has 4,000 pounds of lead in the keel as ballast, while the other has 3,000. Which is the stronger boat? The one with the 3,000-pound keel, because it has 1,000 pounds more fiberglass in the hull.

GRP also has the property of being able to bend or flex somewhat and return to its laid-up shape without fracturing. Once, in the Strait of Juan de Fuca in a fog, my Westsail was lifted up several feet by a swell and dropped on a smooth rock. The interior cabinetry was shoved in about 2½ inches with no damage to the hull. A wooden boat submitted to the same forces would have ended up with fractured planking and frames.

A variation on the solid fiberglass hull is the so-called sandwich hull, which consists of layers of fiberglass, a core of plastic foam, and then more glass layers. Among the advantages of this technology are a quieter and a better-insulated hull. However, the technique is not used much in seagoing yachts as it gives the impression of a sturdiness that is not there.

Of course, for many boatbuilders and cruisers *wood* is still the preferred building material. That affection is based not on safety but on sentiment. There are many wooden boats sailing the world, comfortably taking their owners where they want to go. My favorite—the one I dreamed about long ago—is called a Tahiti ketch. Quite a few were built, and many are still sailing the world. Their popularity derived from their strength and design. Their specifications called for 3-inch-square, steam-bent oak frames set 8 inches apart and 1-inch teak planking. This overbuilding, according to naval architects in the late thirties, would "seriously handicap their speed." But speed is not the objective of the cruiser. Safety and comfort are. I will not otherwise go into details about the merits or deficiencies of wood as a hull material. I would make a lot of enemies among many friends who love their wooden boats. I love wooden boats, too.

Note that *cold-molded* wood hulls are in a very different category from traditional frame-and-plank wood hulls. They are much, much lighter and just as strong as fiberglass for the same thickness. The construction process involves glueing together thin sheets of wood over a frame. The fibers of the wood are crisscrossed, and the result is a fast, lightweight, and strong hull. Friends David and Joan from New Zealand had such a boat, and it was a beauty and fast. We got into a friendly race, just the two boats, sailing north on Chesapeake Bay. I had all our canvas up, and David had his jib partially furled. I knew he loved to go fast, however, so I radioed: "PSYCHE, let her go. I'll see you later in Annapolis." Within a half-hour he was out of sight. By the way, the New Zealanders are fierce competitors in ocean racing.

Steel is my favorite of all hull materials. Early steel hulls were constructed by welding plates together and had a sort of boxy appearance with hard chines. Smooth, finely faired hulls are more efficient for sailing, so with different construction techniques, the boxy look has given way to a smoother, and faster, hourglass shape. I have never had a steel-hulled boat, but for world cruisers with a strong appreciation for safety, I highly recommend the material. I heard about one couple whose steel-hulled boat was tossed up on a coral reef off the east coast of Australia by a vicious storm. When the storm finally wore itself out, they were high and dry, and there was no apparent damage to the hull. With their anchor and chain they winched their boat back across the reef and into deeper water. They continued on their way and a few days later hauled out and checked the hull. Scraped paint was the only evidence that it had ever struck the reef. That's the kind of safety I like now that I am in my advanced years.

Steel has another quality that is useful. It can be repaired anywhere, because welders can be found in even the most primitive regions of the world. If your boat is steel and you don't have space for a generator, take a torch and learn to weld and cut before you go. On a steel hull, rails and lifelines are welded to the hull, not screwed on as with all other boat materials, thus eliminating potential sources of leaks. Other fixtures, such as small-boat davits, towing bits, bowsprits, and boomkins, can also be easily attached permanently. There has to be a catch somewhere, and there is. Steel rusts and attracts condensation. These problems are solved by quick action when they occur. Inside liners keep condensation down. Rust yields to cleaning and the paintbrush. Steel doesn't require more work—all boats require constant maintenance—but it does require more vigilance.

Aluminum has a lot of the advantages of steel and is, of course, lighter. It corrodes more slowly than iron rusts and therefore does not require the constant attention that a ferrous hull does. However, welding is much trickier, and as a consequence, good aluminum welders are harder to find.

Carbon fibers are appearing on the boating scene, but their prohibitively high cost limits their general use in cruising boats to the rigging. Carbon fiber is flexible, lightweight, and strong. Masts of carbon fiber can therefore have a smaller diameter, and thus less windage, than their counterparts in the more traditional materials of wood or aluminum. Carbon fiber shows up in the hulls of modern racing boats, where speed is critical. Other exotic metals, such as *titanium*, are also available but are generally too expensive for any use onboard except fixtures and the like.

Superstructure. The hull, of course, is only part of the boat. The superstructure—the cabin and decks—needs to be as strong as the rest of the boat. The cabin structures of today's fiberglass boats are generally well made and as strong as required for most conditions. The chief threat to their integrity is water—lots of it all at once. One gallon of water weighs 8.35 pounds; imagine now the full weight of huge waves cascading aboard. I can tell you from experience that you want the cabin structure on your boat to be able to withstand the force of a ton or two of solid water. You don't need to be caught by a storm to experience dumping waves, either. Water in a rogue wave, from which no long-distance cruiser is immune, gains speed and power as it curls; tons of water descending on your boat all at once impact with the sound and feel of solid lead. My point is not to frighten you but to emphasize that the superstructure is as important as the hull.

The decks and superstructure of modern fiberglass boats are generally made in the same manner as the hull, either laminated or cored. The cabin structure is built up in a form much as the hull is. The molds have openings for windows, portholes, and companionways and even flanges to attach strengthening bulkheads. Decks are sometimes reinforced. How the deck is joined to the hull also contributes to a boat's structural strength. Be sure you understand the method used on your boat (since this joint can be a source of irksome leaks, this knowledge is doubly useful).

The placement and use of bulkheads also contributes to a boat's strength. Another important factor is where the mast is stepped. Ideally, it is supported directly by the keel, the strongest point on the boat. That is why the mainmast often extends through the cabintop; alternatively, the mast is stepped on the deck with an auxiliary column inside to keep the deck from distorting from the forces acting on the mast.

Windows are a potential Achilles heel, whether they're located in the hull itself or in the cabin structure. Ultimately, what you choose is up to you. The safest are the round portholes normally associated with boats of any size. The weakest are large-sized panes secured with rubber sealant. I have only one recommendation. If the window is close to the water, say less than 4 feet, the standard round porthole is best. We have had waves break against the side of the boat that sounded like solid steel hitting the hull. Small waves of 2 to 4 feet—wind waves superimposed on swells—can occur even in good sailing weather. When the peak of the swell, the curl of the wave, and a gust all arrive at your boat at the same time, the force can be substantial.

Fortunately, the need for strong windows is not frequent; in fact, since the boat is your home, both in port and out, I would opt for wider windows. One of our friends was wrapping up a twelve-year circumnavigation and was just 300 miles from

The Sète (France) boating and fishing club remounts our masts as we prepare to enter the Mediterranean. They ignored my shouted instructions, but the masts finally went up.

home when he encountered his first storm. His only casualty
was a stove-in window. The boat took on a goodly amount of
water before the flow was stanched by stuffing a pillow in the
opening. However, the next day the storm abated, and in the
next port the glass was replaced. In short, I think the size of a
boat's windows is a matter of personal choice: Do you want
more light below and better views from inside the cabin or
maximum safety?

Keel. An important function of the external keel of most small
craft is to provide stability. A potential problem is that the keel
can fall off. The buoyancy of the boat must support the keel's
weight, so the keel must be bolted on. Make sure that the keel
not only fits well but that several bolts holding it are bolted
through to the interior. While it is desirable to find a boat on
which it is possible to check and tighten the bolts, it is difficult; when you look at a boat, at least ask how the ballast is
affixed.

Make sure that the righting moment is quick and strong.
Righting moment is the ability of the boat to right itself when
it has been knocked down (or rolled). When GOLDEN BELL was
knocked down in a 65-knot wind in the North Atlantic, I
knew that Westsails were designed to right themselves, so wasn't
worried (oh yeah?). About three minutes passed before our
mast was again pointing up. We took on water but not an excessive amount; most of it came through the dorades of the
ventilators, which I had foolishly left open (I should have
plugged them with either rags or their lids as soon as the wind
climbed to 30 knots).

Finally, if your boat has a cutaway keel or a spade rudder,
make sure a skeg precedes the rudder. The rudder is a rather
fragile necessity and deserves all the protection that it can get.

Bowsprits and sternsprits. Bowsprits and sternsprits, the extensions of the standing rigging used to give greater sail area to the boat, should be very strong and securely bolted to the hull. I learned how fragile GOLDEN FLEECE's bowsprit was the hard way; I tried to knock down a cofferdam with this 4-inch-thick piece of oak and lost the encounter. The bowsprit was expensive and time-consuming to replace; my carpenter had to hunt far and wide to find a straight-grained piece. The bowsprit on our present Nauticat 38 is welded stainless steel, which we find preferable. Sternsprits of steel offer a good place to hook on a windvane with clamps, instead of through-bolts.

In sum, as you prioritize the features of the right boat for you, don't trade off strength for speed or comfort. And when compromises are necessary, go for comfort over speed, since your boat is to be your home.

3

SAILS AND RIGGING

Older people eventually have to concede that some things in their bodies have changed. Although I was sixty-four when I left for our world-cruising life, I was unaware that I was not as young as I used to be. This egotistic character flaw was subsequently corrected by an event I would have laughed off in earlier years. We were lazying along on a sunny day not far from the equator. We were below when a sudden squall came up. The sails had to come down, and we had no choice but to go up on deck and furl all three—quickly. The jib and staysail were dropped from the cockpit, but the main had to be tugged down from the pitching cabintop. Desperately holding on with one hand, I used the other to fight the big sail down and wrap it on the boom. The task took several minutes. Then the loose foresails had to be gathered in and secured. I was exhausted and suddenly very much aware that I was aging.

THE SAILPLAN AND SAILS

Cruisers have different needs from other sailors. They are touring the world and taking their home with them. Comfort and

29

ease of travel are their priorities. Speed is not; neither is the ability to go to windward. The British nicely capture this attitude in the saying "Gentlemen never sail to windward." The reason we cruisers go west around the world is that in the tropical zones the wind blows in that direction. Of course, we can all go to windward, but doing so requires close hauling and pounding into seas, all the while living on a serious slant. Windward legs are necessary sometimes but to be avoided if possible.

The sailplan. Our second boat, the Westsail 32, was rigged as a ketch. We improved her rigging so that all furling could be done from the cockpit. Our present boat, a Nauticat 38, is also a ketch. Most ketches have four sails: genoa, or foresail; staysail; mainsail; and mizzen. The ketch rig is my favorite sailplan for two reasons. First, the individual sails are smaller because the canvas is divided over four sails. Small means easier to handle. Second, you have a better balance of sails. The mizzen sail is rigged on a short mast well aft and balances nicely with the staysail. We always shortened sail during the night, and this configuration was the way to do it.

One reason that the comfort of a split-rig sailplan is more suitable to seniors than the efficiency of a high-aspect sailplan is that you spend most of your time in harbor and very little under sail. It was almost two years before we left the South Pacific. In that time, including the 34 days we spent reaching the Marquesas, our first landfall in French Polynesia, we spent just 60 days actually at sea. If you have a faster boat, you reach your destination more quickly and have more time to enjoy it. But the difference in speed between a light, fast boat and a heavier, slower divided rig is so small that in a normal passage of two or three days, or even two or three weeks, the gain is not

30

worth the sacrifices in comfort and safety. The point is, for us senior citizens, savings in time are not why we are cruising. We are there to live our lives at a slow pace, to discover and enjoy. What value is a day saved? The only pressing concerns are the seasons. We hurried to arrive at just two places in our ten years of liveaboard cruising: New Zealand and St. Louis, Missouri—New Zealand because summer and the hurricane season were approaching, St. Louis because winter was approaching. Other sailplans have their advocates; the ketch rig is a personal preference of mine.

There are three other sailplans that would, in my opinion, serve senior cruisers well. I have had no experience with them but have had many conversations with those who have. The first is the square rig. Square sails are not efficient going to windward, but they are the best downwind sail you can have. I've seen a number of them on combination rigs, which carry two or three fore-and-aft sails and a high square sail.

The second is the junk rig. Those who have them swear by their ease of handling and furling. I believe all I've heard, in part because they are fully battened, which makes a more efficient air foil. Also, fully battened sails can usually be furled from the cockpit.

The third is the cat rig. This rig has only one mast stepped forward near the bow, and there is usually no standing rigging. On cruising versions of this rig, the sail is dropped into a net of lines strung between a wishbone-shaped boom. The claim is that you don't even have to go outside to furl it. I would like to see how it furls before fully endorsing it, however.

Sails. Unless you have a tough young crew, you may appreciate a yankee jib over a genoa. The yankee is cut with a very high clew. We prefer it for two reasons. First, when the boat is rolling downwind and is sailing wing-and-wing, either with another jib or just the main, the larger sail area higher up is exposed to more wind and the clew and the whisker pole are not apt to dip into the water. Second, the high-cut clew of the yankee allows the crew aft in the cockpit to have clear sight lines forward on the leeward side.

A friend offers another caution, to which I subscribe: "Leave the light-air sails home. They take up a lot of space that could better be used for other things more important to your comfort and safety." Light-air sails are seldom used, are better handled by younger, stronger crew, and are dangerous if a gust or squall comes up. I don't recall ever a time when I wished I had had a spinnaker so the boat could sail faster and reach the next port sooner. You see, I was retired and not in a hurry. Also, a spinnaker and its gear consumes valuable space. Why not use the storage for a couple of folding bicycles instead?

RIGGING

The *standing rigging* consists of the masts and their shrouds. The *running rigging* consists of all the lines that adjust the sails: sheets, furling lines, halyards, and so on. The standing rigging is designed by the boat's naval architect, and except for perhaps substituting stronger cable, should not be altered. The running rigging, however, may require some adjustments to be most compatible with your needs. For most cruisers, the goal is to run all lines to the cockpit. Then the sails can be adjusted without having to go on deck.

Start by installing roller furling everywhere it is possible. Then lead all the lines to the cockpit. You can upgrade the systems yourself or have them installed by a rigger. Add an extra winch or two to provide the power that may be necessary when the wind is strong. Professional riggers and boatyard personnel will have their ideas about winch sizes and types based on formulas and experience. Don't be intimidated! You want bigger winches than are typically installed for your size boat. You want more two-speed winches, too. Consider self-tailing winches and electric winches for lines you use often. And since six or eight lines may terminate in close quarters, you need line stoppers to hold them; cleats are less expensive but not as tidy or as quick and reliable. Talk about line stoppers as though you know what you are talking about. Some lines are difficult to lead to the cockpit, but think twice before you decide to leave them where they are. Get a qualified rigger's opinion before giving up. Swallow your pride and say that pretty soon you are going to be one of the "old geezers" out there. Remember, *you* are the one who will have to go on deck in a heavy shower and 30-knot winds to do whatever must be done.

Roller furling. There are several types of roller furling, and a number of issues for seniors especially to consider. In general, I suggest that you get spools that are oversized for your boat, rather than just right. When the wind is up and you have decided to furl the big genoa, you may not have enough wraps to do it. It has happened to us several times; I invariably then overcompensated the next chance I had to put a few more wraps on the spool, which then fouled the furling line.

There are two ways to solve this problem. One is to purchase roller furling with a continuous line. This requires a special spool-and-line system, but you will never have a foul up from the furling line. I have had no experience with this system but have heard it both praised and derided. The second way is to install the next largest size of furling spool than is specified for your size boat. (In fact, oversizing is a good idea to bear in mind for all deck gear.) The larger size not only makes it possible to put more wraps on the spool but also reduces the force necessary to rotate it.

The furling of the mainsail presents the biggest problem because it is the largest sail and the most difficult to reduce in size. Roller furling is a favorite among cruising sailors but is expensive and, to the purists, reduces the efficiency of the sail. Again I want to ask, "What is your hurry?" Furthermore, if your sail is loose footed, this complaint is not valid. I prefer a loose-footed sail because I think it sets much better than those secured to the boom do.

There are two ways the mainsail can be roller furled. One is to roll it inside the mast. Then, of course, the mast is somewhat "fat," which increases windage. The tack of the sail is at one end of a steel cable that is attached to a gear system that rotates the luff, and the sail furls on itself inside the mast. You have, theoretically, perfect control over the size of the sail, and the sail holds its aerodynamic shape as it is reduced. We have had this feature on our last two boats and have found it quite efficient. There are problems, however, the principal one being that strong or side winds can create folds in the sail, which then prevent the whole sail from being stowed. Our present motor-sailer has the Hood system on both the main and the mizzen. On our previous boat, GOLDEN BELL, the sail furled inside a capsule that screwed to the wooden mast and the furling line was led back to the cockpit. This arrangement worked well in the storm we encountered on the Atlantic.

Another way to get the benefits of this sort of main furling is to install a system that furls the sail just back of the mast but free of any enclosure. This arrangement is my favorite, because it is the least expensive and the strains on the sail in high winds are much less. It has all the furling characteristics of in-the-mast

34

furling, although it lacks the neatness. I wanted to install this kind on GOLDEN BELL in Turkey. The only one on the market at the time was made in Germany. I contacted the factory and was referred to its agent in Italy, who refused to import anything into Turkey because of customs problems with German products. Instead, I took a delivery on a French system with a capsule that screwed to our wooden mast. It could, of course, be pop-riveted to a metal mast.

A third approach involves lazy jacks. In these systems, lines are rigged from the boom to the top of the mast (or close to it). When the main is lowered, the lines gather it around or on top of the boom. This arrangement greatly reduces the confusion of gathering in the mainsail before securing it. The drawback is that you still have to go out on the cabintop and tie the mainsail to the boom. This disadvantage is eliminated in the Doyle StackPack system, which incorporates integral lazyjacks and a cover into a fully battened main.

There are a number of patented furling systems other than the rolling types. We tried only one, and it worked fine when there was no wind. Since the reason for furling is too much wind, we planned to go to lazy jacks but then sold the boat before installing them. I would approach any system cautiously before putting money down. As you may have concluded, I am not much in favor of sail tracks fastening the foot of the sail to the boom and am actually somewhat frightened at the concept of roller furling on the boom. I have experience with both tracks and boom furling and would recommend them only on daysailers and other small boats. They are not for cruisers, since safety is the password for any equipment on the high seas.

Backstays and fittings. You find many cruising boats with double backstays and running backstays. I have no problem with double backstays. Having experienced a backstay failure on GOLDEN FLEECE, our 28-footer, I know how nice it would have been to have had a second to back us up. Only quick action on my part kept the mast from coming down, too, since it was stepped on deck. Had this failure happened during a storm, we would have been in serious trouble. Since that incident, I have rather strongly favored double backstays—and think double forestays may even have merit.

Running backstays are another matter, in my opinion. They were standard equipment in the past when wooden masts were the rule. There are some tremendous forces playing on all masts, but I believe that reefing early and shortening sail are the best ways to reduce the strain. Modern masts are so strong that it is my opinion that running backstays just add weight, windage, and clutter. I have removed them from my boats.

Fixing a temporary backstay in mid-ocean. Note the laundry on the lifelines. Emily calls these "banners of domesticity."

However, before making similar adjustments to your rig, you should consult with a qualified rigger, sail loft, or boat designer to determine which elements of the rigging are essential for your boat.

Finally, you will bless the day you use Norseman-type fittings for your standing rigging. These fittings make it easy for you to replace stays and shrouds. When your standing rigging uses compression fittings, this is not possible. I have had no experience with rod stays, but those whose boats have them praise them.

Remember, it is the sails that move you, the masts that keep them where they do the most good, and the running rigging that creates efficiency in the process. Your rigger should be your best friend, and your sailmaker a close second. Find a book for repairing sails and study it, and take along a sewing machine if you have room.

4

THE CABIN

Selecting an interior for your boat is not much different from selecting a home. You look for, or have designed in, the things that you want. We spent one winter in Barcelona, Spain, where we had a very talented carpenter rebuild the port side of our main cabin. We had purchased GOLDEN BELL in Scotland as is, in spite of several features that we didn't like. We liked the galley, the folding table was terrific, and the navigation table was well designed. But there were four berths in cabin, and the forepeak was rough and used only for storage. Since we traveled alone most of the time, we didn't need four berths. While the former owner had envisioned happy days cruising with fellow bachelors, mostly over long distances, we wanted a comfortable home for the two of us. So we had the two lower berths raised 4 inches and turned into settees. The upper berth on the port side was eliminated in favor of cubbyholes, bookshelves, and small compartments. We turned the forward compartment into a double berth.

These interior modifications made our boat much more attractive, and most important, it suited our needs. We had an

39

extra berth for a guest or crew, the upper starboard. We had privacy forward and a lot more storage places (which promptly filled to capacity as storage places do!). The point is that this boat was our home, and now it was just as we wanted it. Why didn't we get one the way we wanted in the first place? We wanted a Westsail 32, and we wanted to buy it in Europe because we planned to cruise the Mediterranean next. Plus, the Westsails available in Europe at that time were about $10,000 less expensive than those for sale in the United States. We put about half the savings into the remodeling and had an interior that we wanted.

Several books have been written about what makes long-distance liveaboard cruising boats comfortable. Here are some elements of interiors that we found handy, convenient, and comfortable in our cruising years and some that we would have changed.

Galley. The galley should be U shaped. For those times when you go to weather, the stove should be gimbaled and able to move rather freely. Gimbaling the stove also makes downwind sailing less full of surprises. A good arrangement places the stove in the center next to the hull, the sink on the right, and the cold box alongside it toward the hull. The left side has convenient compartments and counter spaces. A three-burner stove is desirable, but two burners are acceptable. Propane is the desired fuel. Do not listen to those who tell you that propane is too dangerous. Nearly all the boats I have been on use it. Propane can be found everywhere in the world. The only supply problems are that the containers are heavy and the refilling stations always seem to be at least a mile away. If your budget is such that you won't be using taxis regularly, invest in a cart. We had what we called a "granny cart," a folding basket with wheels. Finding one can be hard, but it's worth the search. Although it's designed to carry groceries, it's also useful for getting fuel in the remote places where there is no fuel dock. Marine supply stores sell patented folding carts that perform better for these purposes; they are more expensive, of course, but do not rust and have bigger wheels.

Whenever you make an ocean crossing, food storage is a problem (see also chapter 11); I have one caution. Plan on your refrigeration failing. Of course, it probably won't, but if it does, the contents may spoil. If you were counting on the refrigerated goods for most of your meals, you could go hungry. After our 34-day passage to the Marquesas we had enough canned goods left to feed us for two more weeks. I was a crewmember on a

A U-shaped galley. Sink and cold box on the right, gimbaled stove in the center, and shelves and drawers on the left. Stoves should always be gimbaled fore and aft. Sailboats roll much more than they pitch.

passage to Hawaii once, and two weeks out our refrigeration failed. We lost the ice cream, and the cook was planning to throw out the rest of her pre-frozen dinners but was persuaded not to. We had just a few back-up canned goods and fortunately almost made it to the islands before the two bags of ice in the bottom melted. Had a storm blown us far off course we might have had to fish for our suppers.

Refrigeration naturally brings up the subject of insulation. The standard for most refrigerators on well-made cruising boats is 4 inches of foam insulation. The skipper for whom I was crewing to Hawaii had built the boat himself and figured that if 4 inches were good, 6 inches were better. I cannot recommend too strongly having adequate insulation. The so-called portable refrigerators do not pass muster with their 1- to 2-inch insulation.

Navigation station. Having a decent place to navigate is vital. Charts and tables need to be quickly accessible, well organized, and well lit. (Well lit means also having a red light to study the chart at night, so you don't lose your night vision.) For chart storage, I prefer having a flat drawer that accepts folded charts, but some cruisers like storing their charts rolled up. I find the rolls waste space and the charts difficult to lay flat. A pencil sharpener is essential. I know that you can sharpen pencils with a sharp knife, but somehow you end up with more curses than sharp points. Another tip is to keep an emery board handy to sharpen the lead. You need also to stow the tools of navigation neatly and ready at hand. Your navigation center needs to have all the instruments easily accessible at a glance.

When we were in New Zealand an American yacht competing in the Whitbread-Round-the-World Race stopped in the

The Cabin

Bay of Islands and invited visitors to come aboard. The interior was pretty spartan. Pipe berths ranged along the hull, and a small area contained an efficient galley and dining table that seated four. There was nothing else in the interior—except a navigation center that was enclosed, was heated, and had a well-padded leather armchair that faced a row of instruments, monitors, dials, and switches. I was reminded of the captain's chair on the Starship ENTERPRISE. Obviously, the racers considered the navigation center of extreme importance. You ought to, also.

Main saloon. Usually in boats less than 50 feet long, the general living and dining areas are combined in the main saloon. Many ingenious interior arrangements have been designed by naval architects, and they all seem to work quite well. It is usually true that the best location for the saloon is the lowest and most central spot in the hull. Other than recommending that it have sufficient handholds and rounded corners, I can only suggest getting a boat that appeals the most to you. Then be happy with the one you select and emphasize its seaworthiness over features you miss. It is said that you always buy three boats with any purchase: the one you wanted, the one you bought, and the one you wish you had gotten.

Berths. Berth arrangements are largely personal choices. However, if you want a double bunk, there is an advantage to sleeping crosswise to the boat; at sea, and especially in a storm, you sleep better. We have not had that feature in our boats (although it was available from the factory). We have, in storms, braced ourselves crosswise with pillows and slept quite well. But remember, storms are to be avoided when possible and endured on the rare occasion when not and thus constitute a very small part of your living-aboard time. It may be far better to brace yourself for a couple of nights and then have a convenient and comfortable time in an anchorage or marina than to design your boat only for passages.

Lighting. On our boats, we have replaced most of the incandescent lights with fluorescent lights. They give more light and use less electricity. If you read in bed, and older people tend to do a lot of that, wire separate reading lights for each sleeper. Small fluorescent strip lights mounted behind a valance provide excellent light for the galley counter. We have one oil lamp that hangs in our saloon, but it generates more heat than light; we use it only on cold days to convince guests that we are really salty.

Heads. Most heads are quite efficiently designed. I can recommend systems that macerate and chemically treat waste before discharge, although they do consume more space in the head and require chemicals and electricity to operate. Be aware that many ports around the world are quite strict about discharge. Shower water and dishwater, so-called gray water, have not been a problem anywhere we have cruised.

Closets and storage. For liveaboard cruisers, the more storage the boat has, the better. A hanging locker for the owners is almost essential. Most boats have one, although often the locker is only half-length and suitable just for garments that stop or begin at the waist. The more drawers there are, the better. It is much easier to get to small items in drawers than in under-seat compartments. See if a good cabinetmaker can't replace some of those storage areas under seats with pullout drawers. You lose some overall space but gain in usefulness. Besides, for seniors, more is not better, but easier is. And finally, if you are re-configuring lockers, drawers, and shelving, remember that books, in aggregate, are heavy and that heavier objects are better placed lower than higher.

One type of storage that is a big problem *when needed* is a wet locker, the place where you store your foul-weather gear when you come below in a storm. Very few boats under 50 feet have such a luxury. The allocation of space to this purpose requires special design and of course plenty of ventilation and perhaps a drip into the bilge. We store our wet gear in the forward head. If you have two heads, you're lucky; otherwise designate some place where the wet gear can be hung temporarily to drip for a few minutes. A dedicated wet locker on a small boat is inefficient use of space.

Bilge. Don't forget to consider the boat's bilge. Most mental pictures of the bilge feature a cavity full of foul-smelling, oily slosh. I have never had such a bilge, but because one might grow on me without warning, I make an effort to quickly wipe up any oil and fuel spills and pour in sweet-smelling cleaners. As a result, we have used our bilge mainly to store beer and soft drink cans and infrequently used canned goods. They fared well and were at a suitable temperature when brought out. Mark the top of canned goods with a permanent marker and remove any paper labels. The bilge is also a good place to store extra galvanized chain. We store our take-down anchor there also. (The lower in the boat heavy items are, the better it is for recovery in knockdowns.)

As you consider different interior arrangements, don't despair. You will not find the ideal boat. As you do with spouses, you live with what you get—none are perfect. If you want a custom boat, hire a naval architect, be clear that the boat is to used as a liveaboard home, not for weekend cruises or daysailing, and specify that comfort is a main criterion, not speed or ability to sleep large numbers.

5

SAFETY, SAFETY HARDWARE, AND SAFETY EQUIPMENT

W hether you're at sea or in port, most cruising boat accidents occur on deck. And like most accidents of any kind, anywhere, they can be avoided. Prudent mariners have the benefit of experience and history to help them anticipate many common accidents. Emily and I have had no serious incidents, but we have had a few misses that were potentially serious, some that were just annoying, and a few that were hilarious. When you are equipping your boat and preparing for long-distance cruising and living aboard, consider how to add safety features to minimize problems and increase comfort.

Safety, so the safety experts say, is a state of mind. This state of mind encompasses the prevention factor. It is a state of mind that causes you to insist that lines are coiled and secured, loose items are stowed, cotter keys are in place, and all knots are snugged up before you leave port. "Shipshape and Bristol fashion" is the phrase often used to describe this kind of attention to detail.

BELOWDECKS

While most cruising accidents happen topsides, there are some problems that occur belowdecks. Let's deal with those first. The pitch and roll of a boat is steady and unpredictable. Because people's balance generally deteriorates with age, seniors cannot always handle the abrupt and unpredictable nature of the boat's motion. For this reason the interior must have a lot of handholds. When the seas kick up a bit, I resort to moving hand-over-hand, Tarzan fashion, never releasing my grip from one point of contact until I have touched the next. Also, put fiddles on the edges of tables, counters, and shelves to make them easier to grasp as well as to keep items in place. Keep doors on cabinets closed when underway so you aren't hit by flying objects. We have lost a bit of crockery by not doing so. Incidentally, do not suppose that because you are in a river or protected sound you do not have these problems. 'Tain't so! Many powerboaters seem to delight in roaring past sailboats and rocking them with a heavy wake.

Once, on the Tombigbee River in Mississippi, we were rocked by a large powerboat whose wake was the equivalent of the worst surges we had experienced on the oceans. At the next lock, we heard that the boat's wake had also overturned a small fishing boat, dumping the occupants in the water. It had been reported by radio to the lockmaster, who detained the boat; the operator was fined several hundred dollars. That happy ending doesn't occur very often. Every sailor has similar stories to tell, so keep things secured in the cabin and, of course, on deck.

ON DECK

Abovedecks, the greatest safety features of a sailboat are the handrails and lifelines. Your boat should have strong lifelines.

Safety, Safety Hardware, and Safety Equipment

If there are no bulwarks, three lifelines are better than two. On GOLDEN FLEECE I even rigged a fourth line, using ⅜-inch line secured at the boat's ends but draped to the shrouds. I wanted something in addition to my harness to catch me if a roll tossed me off the cabintop. Lifelines increase in value by height and strength of the stanchions. Stanchions welded to a steel hull are strongest; those bolted through the deck are the next strongest. Netting tied to the steel cables of the lifelines and sturdy ropes laced to them increase safety, especially for children and dogs.

Bulwarks are another important safety feature, although true bulwarks are not seen on many production boats. On long-distance cruising boats they not only help provide security for the crew, but also prevent items meant to stay aboard from leaving. Tools dropped on the deck won't roll overboard if bulwarks are in the way. Bulwarks also partially protect items lashed to the lifelines from assault by solid water. The only disadvantages to bulwarks are that they increase windage and the boat's cost. In my opinion, their value outweighs the additional expense. I'm not alone: I have seen many cruising boats with bulwarks added by savvy sailors who place comfort and safety above their boat's "design lines."

Most accidents occur on deck because that is where the action is. Many sailors take great pride in keeping their boat shipshape. On a shipshape boat, all ropes are coiled and secured. All items on deck are lashed down and put in a place where they do not slide. Sails are securely lashed or in bags. Sailbags are stowed below once the sails are removed. The furling line of roller-furled sails is secured by a line stopper or secured to a cleat with a half-hitch. (I once watched a genoa flog to shreds in a nearby marina during a storm because its furling line was left loose.) Neatness helps prevent accidents.

I call staysail booms widow-makers. All our boats have been cutter rigged, and the staysail on each was set on a boom. As I was preparing GOLDEN FLEECE for the Pacific crossing, I found that, when we tacked, I had to go forward several times to ease the genoa around the babystay. As a boat moves through the wind, there's a short period when the sails flog, including the staysail on its boom, which thrashes about wildly. I was clobbered twice, and once I thought the boom had broken my forearm. I finally asked myself two questions: What good is a staysail? and, Does a staysail need a boom? The staysail is useful for going to weather, shortening sails in a storm, and heaving-to, so I took off the boom. The boat sailed nearly as well when the wind was forward of the beam. With the wind

Paul seated on deck. a) The ropes connecting the fore and aft lower shrouds are a way of getting aloft much in the manner of old vessels. b) A boarding ladder can be used both with the dinghy and for swimming. c) A web strap is attached to the harness.

aft of the beam the staysail mostly rippled in stalled wind, which it always did, boom or not. I left the boom at home when I departed. I have removed every boom almost immediately after taking possession of the new boats.

A number of devices can increase the safety of the crew on deck, either by helping prevent accidents or by preventing an accident that occurs from becoming a tragedy. The most important is a safety harness. Emily and I wear our harnesses whenever we're sailing on large straits and, of course, on the open ocean. You should have no problem finding one that fits comfortably from among the many on the market. Your boat should carry one harness for each crewmember. A harness has no value as a lifesaver if it is not worn, however, or if the person wearing it does not fasten on to a strong point on the boat.

I have two recommendations with respect to "strong points." The first is to attach a strong steel cable to the forward mooring cleat and run it back to the after mooring cleat. These are the two strongest fixtures on deck. The cable should run inboard of the shrouds and lifeline stanchions; then, when you come on deck, you can snap onto the cable and go forward or aft the full length of the boat without having to unsnap. If the task you're trying to accomplish requires you to snap on elsewhere, wait until the roll of the boat is favorable before unhooking from the cable. In general, any line, such as a sheet, does not make a good attachment point. The standing rigging is secure, however. Lifelines are adequate, although harness manufacturers advise against using them, because they can be too small and can rust to weakness. In addition to installing a deck-length cable, I recommend adding a strong padeye just at the entrance to the cabin. We had a rule on our boat: When at sea, thou shalt not go on deck without your harness on and snapped onto the padeye.

51

Three personal experiences may explain why we insisted on adhering to the rule. I was pitched overboard in the South Seas. I was wearing my harness and not concerned about being in the water. The harness turned me over, and the boat pulled me through the water but in a proper position. I had learned my lesson from an earlier passage to Hawaii, where an emergency arose on the boat I was crewing on, and the captain rushed on deck without his harness. His wife yelled for him to put on his harness, but she was ignored. "You said nobody was to go up on the deck without a harness. You just did!" she angrily spit out when he came back below. I went out on deck (wearing my harness) and waited for the storm to subside. The point is that a rogue wave could easily have swept him over the side. She would have lost a husband, and I would have lost a navigator and friend. Furthermore, I was just learning celestial navigation and doubt if I could have hit our island. In the Atlantic, we nearly duplicated my South Seas experience; we were caught by a fierce storm, and since we were in the shipping lanes, we had to keep watch at all times. A rogue wave doused the man on deck, and he started to slide toward the rail. His harness stopped him before he slid under the lifelines and into the ocean.

One device to help those with balance problems is a brace that can be bolted to the cabintop near the main mast. This hip-height, three-legged affair made of stainless steel pipe gives someone working at the mast something to press against if both hands are needed for some critical task. Although you are tied on by your harness, you can still be thrown across the deck by a sudden lurch. This device prevents you from being launched in the first place.

Unfortunately, tethers themselves can cause accidents by getting caught on deck projections (you snag, you become irritated, you unsnap, and whoosh!). A two- or three-legged piece

52

of stainless rod covering major projections can reduce the potential for accidents by allowing any line to ride up and over the obstruction.

Another item I particularly recommend that senior cruisers have rigged and ready on deck is a four-part block and tackle, sometimes called a handy-billy. It should be capable of extending to 10 feet. Use ¼- or ⅜-inch line with a soft lay; you need 60 feet all together. Put a cam cleat on one of the blocks and snap-shackles on both ends. This device has multiple uses; it can help break out a stubborn anchor or be employed as an adjustable preventer for the main boom. The most useful purpose I can think of is hauling aboard an exhausted or unconscious person, a task that may not present too great a problem for younger cruisers, but could be impossible for us oldsters.

IN THE WATER

Suppose that, despite your best precautions, an accident does occur, and the cry that strikes terror in the hearts of every sailor goes out, "Man overboard!" It's difficult to spot someone in the water when the seas are calm, almost impossible when whitecaps are present, and certainly impossible at night. A man-overboard pole—ready to toss immediately—is absolutely essential on a cruising boat. Consisting of a small float pierced by a long pole with a flag on one end and a weight on the other, this device gives you a visible target to return to. Floating strobe lights and horseshoe rings are tethered to some models, and there are devices that dump the entire assembly into the water with the yank of a cord. If you are going to sail on the open ocean, get one. You could be the one in the water watching your boat's stern disappear while your crew hunts for you.

Now suppose that when you reach the person in the water,

he or she is strong enough to climb out unassisted. There must be some way to climb aboard! Some boats carry a rolled rope ladder for this purpose; others hang a rope from the bottom rung of a hinged steel or aluminum ladder so someone in the water can flip the ladder down. When I was preparing my boat for cruising, I slowly swam around it, reaching up to see if I could grab a handhold somewhere. I discovered that just having a handhold would not get me on board. When I was young, I could chin myself twenty times. Now, I need a place to put a foot to help hoist my weight to deck level. I solved the problem by putting a folding mast step on the large rudder. The increased water friction was a small price to pay for a life. Whatever system you design or buy, test it!

However, if the person in the water can't climb out unassisted, hook up the handy-billy described above or deploy your Lifesling, a manufactured device that serves the same recovery function. Probably the most common life-saving aid seen on cruising sailboats, it is available in different sizes from the major marine suppliers. We have had one ever since it was brought to market; I've tested it—it works. Many books cover man-overboard procedures in depth, and you should read several. Since you cannot survive chilly or cold water as long as you used to, you should plan in advance for this possibility.

Do not go to sea without the distress signaling device known as an EPIRB (emergency position indicating radio beacon). Consider this scenario: You have abandoned your boat and watched it sink beneath the sea. Huddled in your liferaft you and your crew look at each other—now what? Your last position showed you 500 miles from the nearest land. You see nothing but water. No boats, nothing! You are about as lonely as you will ever be. You remember that you should have activated your EPIRB as you entered the raft, and you do so immediately. A radio signal begins flooding the atmosphere for hundreds of miles, reaching ships, passing airplanes, and satellites. All nations of the world are a part of this emergency network. About two hours later a plane flies overhead and drops a package. The chances are good that you will spend the night in a berth on a big ship that has been diverted to rescue you. You really were not alone; you had your EPIRB with you. There have been many advances in marine electronics recently. Get the latest at your marine store.

Establishing an abandon-ship routine must also be part of your pre-cruise preparations. This routine should be practiced several times initially and once or twice a year thereafter. A life-raft is an obvious prerequisite; the good ones are expensive but less expensive than your life. One of their most valuable features is that they provide protection against the weather. Because the rafts contain supplies enough for only a few days, your procedure should include offloading an abandon-ship bag, which should contain extra food, a very sharp clasp knife, a flare gun, extra cartridges, fishing supplies, and a VHF hand-held radio (which you need to remember to keep charged). Many more items can be suggested, and each skipper has his or her favorite list of necessaries. Just as essential as the bag is a supply of water; this is why most yachts stow extra 5-gallon jugs of fresh water on deck. When you abandon ship, cut the lines loose, provide some means of keeping the jugs in sight, and throw them overboard—or toss them into the raft or dinghy, if you've had time to launch the tender as well. Marine supply stores also stock hand-operated watermakers and solar stills that fit nicely in an abandon-ship bag. Investigate these options if you are going to cross an ocean.

Abandoning ship is something that few cruisers want to think about, but mentally rehearse your procedures often. Do not waste time on trivialities. Your wedding ring on the lavatory, passports, money, and credit cards are all important when the boat is afloat. First do those things that are important when it's sinking: launch the liferaft and dinghy, offload the fresh water and abandon-ship bag, scoop up spare food and extra clothing if it is chilly; only then consider gathering up the other things that are precious to you.

However, if the water is not coming up fast, try to find and stop the leak first. Try bailing as a way to stay afloat. There should always be plenty of buckets aboard and handy. You should decide to abandon ship only when there is no other alternative. A Northwest boat sprang a leak during a race to Hawaii many years ago. Prior to leaving, the skipper had been shopping for some touch-up paint when he saw a stack of plastic buckets. On impulse he bought them. He had a lot of young crew who bailed furiously for several hours until they found the leak and fixed it. It has often been said that "there is no bilge pump quite as fast as a scared man with a bucket."

Another abandon-ship story with a powerful message comes out of an around-England race a few years ago. A very bad storm sprang up, and many boats took on water. Several crews took to their liferafts. When the storm stopped, an empty raft was found floating upside down, while the boat to which it belonged was found floating upright with no one aboard. The crew all perished. The moral here is plain: Make very sure that your boat is sinking before you leave it. There are many ways of stopping a leak; try them first—but don't stop preparing to abandon ship.

ALOFT

Sooner or later you have to go up the mast, whether you like it or not. If you have a young crewmember aboard who is mechanically inclined, he or she should go up. The problem is that you don't always know what the problem aloft is and what to do about it. If you've sailed much you know what I mean. Most long-distance cruisers, including myself, feel that mast steps are more than just a convenience, they're nearly a necessity. For aged cruisers, they are a necessity. Even with good two-speed winches, it is not easy to hoist a 150- to 200-pound man up the mast, young or old. And if you are a cruising couple, the stronger and heavier of the two may be the one sent aloft. Unless you have internal halyards, I strongly suggest that you do a lot of investigating before deciding which mast step system to install. GOLDEN BELL had folding mast steps, which I ordered from the factory in Canada, and I was more than satisfied with them. On GOLDEN FLEECE, our Pacific crossing boat, the steps were heavy-gauge aluminum strips that I pop-riveted to the mast. The halyards fouled occasionally, but we lived with it. Incidentally, having steps on the mast does not mean that you can go aloft without a harness. Attach the harness to a halyard and have your crew take a couple of turns around the biggest winch on the mast; should you slip off the steps, the halyard and harness will break or stop your fall. Be sure to use the harness at the marina as well as at sea, as boat wakes can roll the boat as easily as waves.

There are other ways of going aloft, of course. Larry Pardey, one of the best and most self-sufficient sailors I know, swears by a block-and-tackle system he uses; you can hoist yourself up without any help. However, it is more than this old salt can handle; it requires that you pull every inch of a 300-foot rope through four blocks! I noticed that Pardey used a wraparound bosun's chair just so that he would stay in the chair if he lost control of the bitter end of the hoist rope.

A bosun's chair is still the most common device used to the

top of the mast. Why? If you have to go up, you might as well be sitting down when you get there. But somebody has to get you up there, and that means having one crew, possibly two, on deck and having a strong winch on the mast. There ought to be a law requiring one over-sized, two-speed winch on every mast. If you don't have one, try to have one installed. Then buy the longest winch handle available. If you can figure out a way to run the lines, your anchor winch may substitute for the mast winch.

Look around your boat. If you see anything that might cause an accident, stow it, tie it down, or get rid of it. Remember Murphy's law. Repeat these steps every day, because safety is really a state of mind.

6

PILOTING, SEAMANSHIP, AND NAVIGATION

Piloting is essentially the process of running the boat. To do so successfully you must get from Point A to Point B without incident. To do that requires that you know where you are at all times and what lies ahead. But trying to anticipate and prepare for all challenges and difficulties may actually impede successful voyaging, so this chapter suggests issues that you as a senior cruiser might want to think about or understand better. Weather is a good example. Younger sailors just set out when they have the time to go; they take whatever weather is their lot. The mature sailor plans the voyage to avoid bad weather.

Detailed how-to discussions of piloting and navigation are found in many good books. My first suggestion is that you beg, borrow, or buy a copy of *Chapman Piloting, Seamanship, and Small Boat Handling,* by Elbert S. Maloney, the bible of piloting for many years. Because its coverage is very detailed, it is not a reference you can pull off the bookshelf and refer to for the first time when you are already in trouble. To supplement the book and your own on-the-water practice, you might also take a navigation course, such as those offered by the Coast Guard auxiliary, power squadrons, yacht clubs, and community colleges. Many of these study courses use Chapman as their text or premier reference.

On the Erie Canal, steering from the after deck.

Piloting, Seamanship, and Navigation

Successful piloting isn't necessarily difficult, but it does require thought. An example from my own experience explains what I mean. We were sailing north the full length of the coast of Washington State, from the Columbia River entrance to Neah Bay, an overnight trip. I had stood my watch and was followed by someone who had taken his own boat up the same coast several times. I was snoring, peacefully I think, when two hours later his relief awakened me, "Paul, I think you had better check us out. I think we may be headed for trouble." A quick assessment of radar and depthsounder showed that we were about a mile from shore and headed directly for an offshore island. I quickly ordered that the helmsman steer due west for 2 miles, then resume our northerly course, staying 3 miles off the shore, including islands. The previous watchstander had assumed that my order to "stay on course" meant maintain compass course, even though I had told him to keep 3 miles offshore using the radar. My point is that all helmsmen are pilots and must always be given latitude to steer a safe course. The old adage that you do not change course (compass) without the permission of the captain has probably wrecked not a few vessels. Make sure your crew understands this distinction. Close attention to the compass is important only out of sight of land where there is nothing to run into.

In the Pacific Northwest, my home waters, helmsmen worry more about depth readings than course, since rocks form the bottom of many a passage. In coastal waters, develop the habit of glancing at the depthsounder every 20 or 30 seconds. In East Coast waterways it's often the only way you can stay in the channels in the canals and rivers. We older sailors tend to get a little drowsy after lunch, but nothing snaps you awake like seeing a reading of 7 on the depthsounder when your boat draws 6 feet.

Charts, of course, are essential to navigation, because they illustrate what physical objects exist in the waters you're sailing. Charts, especially where to get them and which to buy, worry a lot of sailors. You can learn to read them very quickly; all the symbols are explained in chart number 1. In the United States, the government publishes charts for both local and foreign waters (through different agencies); Canadian and British charts are also readily available. When you are ready to be serious about your cruising dream and have a boat (not necessarily world class yet), you can profit immensely from having a friendly conversation with your local (or Internet) chart agent.

Here are a few thoughts concerning charts from our experiences and those of others. Charts are available almost anywhere in the world in large or moderately large cities. Also, since you must check in with customs and immigration whenever you reach a new country, you arrive in known ports where there is more than likely to be a marine supply store. The inventory of these stores mostly likely won't approach that of a West Marine or Boat US store, and you may not find any charts in English, but with local help you can figure out where the rocks and shallow places are. We had some U.S. charts for the Mediterranean but found the Greek charts much more helpful after we learned the meaning of most of the words.

Cruisers are another source of local charts overseas. Ask around the anchorage. Offer to trade some of yours. And if you are a naval officer or retired military, you should check with any military vessels in the harbor. One friend acquired a complete set of Mediterranean charts from a naval tug that had just received all new up-to-date charts from the United States. The old ones were about to be burnt when he requested permission to board and asked about their disposal.

We found that charts weren't necessary when we were

crossing open ocean; we substituted inexpensive crosshatched paper. We just marked the latitude and longitude for each square and then drew a straight line from Point A to Point B. Emily was the ship's official "dot maker"; crossing the Pacific, we watched her position fixes crawl across the paper as we approached New Zealand. I admit that for part of that passage the navigation materials may not have been precise, but we raised our landfall only 15 minutes off our predicted time.

You do need coastal charts, archipelago charts, and harbor charts. With charts costing upwards of $16 each, however, purchasing all that you anticipate needing could be quite expensive. Charts are also unnecessary in much of the world. Some areas are very adequately covered in cruising guides—books that include charts of harbors and anchorages, the location of marinas, and a host of other information that's useful once you arrive. I used *Charlie's Charts* in the South Pacific. For each archipelago covered, the guide gave detailed information about passes though the reef, anchorages, marinas, and customs locations as well as such local information as history, taboos, and places to visit or purchase groceries. The islands were carefully drawn, including land profiles as you approached from the four cardinal directions. It's worth adding a few such guidebooks to your ship's library before you leave home waters.

Of course, they're also available at your destinations. For example, chart stores and marine supply stores all over Europe carry guides for several of the seas, the Spanish coast, the Turkish coast, and everywhere cruisers venture. If you want to tackle the French canals—and you will be well rewarded if you do—you should know that the French government prints detailed guides for every navigable kilometer. Detailed charts are also available for all navigable rivers and canals in the United States; Emily and I took SUNSET up the East Coast and then through the

Erie Canal, Great Lakes, and many rivers of America's heartland. We can certainly recommend that trip for those who shrink from high-seas adventures. The point is that you don't have to acquire everything you need before you leave home.

Electronic navigation has become very sophisticated and has many exciting facets. The satellite-based global positioning system (GPS), which was developed by the military, is a great gift to seamen. Using a small GPS unit that fits in your hand, you can determine your position to within 100 meters anywhere in the world. (Military equipment receives position information accurate to within 1 meter. The signal is downgraded for civilian use.) The Coast Guard, who seem a bit more conscious of their responsibilities to the public than some government agencies, have set up conversion stations, similar to Loran stations, that convert your GPS signals to

A night stop on the French canals. Charolais cattle was grazing near by and the tinkle of the cow bells lulled us to sleep.

about a 12- to 15-meter accuracy. You must be in range of one of these land-based stations for the conversion to work. Check with your local marine electronic store to see if you are likely to be cruising in a covered area.

The latest spectacular advance in navigation is to integrate a laptop computer, a GPS, and electronic outputs from your other instruments. With these inputs the computer can steer the boat for days without your having to touch the controls. I have seen such technology, but in my advanced years find it a toy— lots of fun to play with, but not essential. A significant flaw in such a system is that it doesn't watch out for other boats. Besides, steering the boat and keeping watch is an element of cruising that I like. The water, the vast distances that open up, the constant scanning of the horizon for other vessels, the adjustments to the helm (yes, we have an autopilot), the wildlife that passes—all enfold me in the environment that is a part of my lifelong dream. Perhaps it's part of yours, too.

For senior cruisers, autopilots are essential. The "tyranny of the helm" is a fact, and any relief from it is not only welcome, but also sometimes necessary. In the canals of France where autopilots wouldn't work, I stood hour after hour facing the canal ahead while grasping the tiller behind me and consequently developed cramps in my legs and back. Fortunately, Emily could relieve me occasionally.

Speaking of relief, without some kind of self-steering, you cannot go to the head or pour a new cup of coffee if your mate is asleep or otherwise not available. Regarding relief "over the rail," there is a saying among cruisers that most men found floating face down in the sea had their flies open. Remember the sailor's adage "One hand for yourself, one hand for the boat." It is never more important than when performing this bodily function.

If you plan to cross oceans and your sailboat is less than 50 feet long another essential item is a steering vane. There are many versions and designs, all of which work. The principle is simple enough: The vane keeps the boat at a constant relationship to the wind. When you have steady winds, such as in the trades, a steering vane can keep you on a constant compass course for days, untiring, alert to the slightest attempt to change the course, and demanding not one watt of electrical energy. If you are on dead reckoning, and of course you are, you need to check the compass regularly, as it is the only way you have of knowing you are still on course.

Now, please raise your right hand and repeat after me, "I solemnly swear that I will not go to sea unless I know celestial navigation and have a sextant on board." You don't have to be good at celestial, and you can save yourself with simple noon sights or sun sights. Your sextant will never run out of batteries, but your GPS and calculator might. Make a habit of checking your chronometer and wristwatch with the radio daily. With celestial and an accurate timepiece, you can go anywhere in the world without concern. Emily and I used to take a sun sight at least every other day during passages just to keep in shape.

A great fear that ocean cruisers have is being run down at sea by a huge ship. Two basic facts bear emphasizing. First, a large, quickly moving cargo vessel can come from below the horizon to your position in 15 minutes. The crew on watch must sweep the horizon every 15 minutes. We kept a small kitchen timer on board so that when it was necessary to stay below, we were able to time the 15-minute intervals carefully. Second, a large ship is undoubtedly on autopilot, and especially at night, the watch on the bridge is sleepy, bored, and may not even care if the ship should run down a small boat. Furthermore, it is not possible for a large ship to stop quickly or even turn enough to avoid you. You should do all you can to stay out of *its* way.

At night the direction a ship is moving is easily determined by noting the arrangement of the all-around white lights, which are positioned so they are not obscured by any part of the vessel. The forward light is lower than the after light. When the ship is to your right and the lower light appears to the right of the upper light, for example, the ship is no threat. If the ship is to your left and the lower light is to the right, you may be on a collision course. A bit of playing with a small model or analyzing diagrams can sharpen your perceptions and relieve a lot of nighttime anxiety. Until you get good at reading the lights, however, wake the skipper to confirm your observation.

Radar is very useful, especially when fog closes out the rest of the world beyond the rail. It enables you to stay a certain

A beautiful day at sea. Paul shoots the sun for a running fix.

distance offshore if you are traveling along a coast. It also detects other vessels in the area at night and even fishermen in small boats if they have reflective materials. Hanging a radar reflector high in your rigging is added insurance to make your boat show up on someone else's radar. (You still show up as just a blip on the other vessel's screen—if its radar is on; many large vessels depend more on lights than radar to detect nearby craft.)

We once had to navigate across the Gulf of Mexico at night with very low batteries. The compass light was not working, and neither was the autopilot. To hold a flashlight on the compass and steer is very tiring. It was then that I learned to steer by the stars. Pick out a star near the horizon that's on your compass course and steer for it. Of course, stars rise and set, but check the compass frequently and pick out a new one when necessary.

Have you ever wondered how the Polynesians populated much of the Pacific? This was a source of wonder to me until I read a book called *We, The Navigators* by David Lewis. In it, Lewis describes the navigation principles and methods the Polynesian seafarers used to travel great ocean distances, relying on their abilities to read the stars, wind, waves, and natural phenomena. That kind of information can be useful to you, too. The book makes fascinating reading and helps attune you to the subtleties of the ocean environment. There are other books on this subject as well; the traditional navigation arts of the Polynesians are also being preserved by the Hawaii-based Polynesian Voyaging Society, which sponsors expeditions by the huge voyaging canoe HOKULE'A throughout the Pacific. A replica of a traditional Polynesian ocean-going canoe, HOKULE'A arrived in New Zealand while we were there, and the Maoris, the native people of New Zealand, sent out their ceremonial canoe to meet it. We watched the ceremony from our boat; it was a spectacular experience.

7

WEATHER

by Harry Mitchell

Weather is one navigational issue that concerns all sailors. We all soon learn that there are certain times when you don't cross open seas. For example, I reached Cabo San Lucas, at the southern tip of Baja Mexico, at Christmas time. My arrival had been planned so that I would have time to prepare the boat for the long passage to the Marquesas and then be able to set off during the most favorable time—that is, when the chances of bad storms on the route were minimal. Also, the trip down the entire West Coast of the United States needs to be made in a favorable season. Fall storms in the Pacific Northwest are to be avoided. Certain capes in California need to be rounded swiftly, and you must wait patiently for the right weather window. All of these bits of advice I learned from other sailors, locals, and weather experts in Portland before I left.

At Cabo ten or fifteen boats were waiting to depart. We had a meeting of all those headed for the South Seas. Some were going in February, some in March. Nobody was leaving in January; the winter storms in the Northern Hemisphere were still a threat. In mid-February

I decided to go. I did not have Jimmy Cornell's *World Cruising Routes* to guide me (it had not been written yet), but there was a lot of experience around that table that December day. We were told that by March most of the Northern Hemisphere storms would be over and by the time we got into the Southern Hemisphere the hurricane season would be about over there, too. This is weather planning.

All of the information we had and communicated to each other is public knowledge and contained in many charts, graphs, books, and papers. Ferreting it out and organizing it into something approaching comprehensibility can be a Herculean task. If you have a fascination

The day before departure from Cabo San Lucas, Mexico for the Marquesas in French Polynesia.

70

with complex diagrams, try to get the pilot charts for whatever sections of the ocean interest you.

In 1988 Emily and I had planned to cross the Atlantic with about 250 other cruisers in an event organized by Jimmy Cornell. We were all to meet in the Canary Islands by December, when the fleet was scheduled to leave. Why December? The southern tradewinds start to blow during that month. It was suggested that we leave for the Canaries in August or September and enjoy some time in these tropical isles. Why August or September? The North Atlantic storms begin in the fall. We couldn't make the passage that soon, and we actually didn't depart Gibraltar until November 1. Several locals in Gibraltar suggested we might run into a little weather, but we left full of hope in good weather. Two days later we were hove-to in 30 knots of wind. Seven days later, after being knocked down in 65 knots, we turned tail and returned to Spain. It took 10 days for that storm to blow out. We just had bad luck. Cornell's book suggests that the passage be made no later than October and his letter to the cruising fleet recommended an even earlier departure—good advice, as it happened!

Only fools climb in their boats and take off for opposite shores without checking the weather. When I took flying lessons quite a few years ago a slogan on the wall read, "There are foolish pilots, and old pilots, but there are no foolish old pilots." May I introduce you to an "old" pilot who ended his sailing career with a perfect passage from New Zealand to the Strait of Juan de Fuca in Washington State? We first met Harry and Marge Mitchell on ham radio. Harry was running a net devoted to weather that was of great value to those of us in the Western Pacific. He rose early every morning, took the international weather data by code, and prepared his forecast in time for the net at 0800. We have kept in touch, and although they did one foolish thing (trading their beautiful sailboat, WHALESONG, for a ranch in Montana), Harry lost none of his weather savvy. Therefore, I asked him what weather advice he would give to senior cruisers; he wrote the following. —PHK

Many publications are available to guide sailors in forecasting weather and relating existing conditions to what can be expected to happen next. My purpose here is to guide cruisers towards a safe and efficient passage by giving them an idea of what to look for in the weather forecasts they get by radio and e-mail.

Cyclonic winds around a low are of the most interest to sailors expecting bad weather. These systems are generally referred to as lows and vary in intensity from shallow lows to full-blown hurricanes. Cyclonic winds of hurricane strength are called by different names according to the ocean in which they are found. In the North Atlantic they are called hurricanes; in the Northwest Pacific, typhoons; and in the Southwest Pacific, cyclones. Wherever they are, you do not want to be there at the same time unless you and your boat are tucked into a safe hurricane hole.

In the Northern Hemisphere winds rotate around lows in a counterclockwise direction. In the Southern Hemisphere the winds rotate clockwise around the center of the low. This distinction is important and should be kept in mind by those crossing the equator. The converse of a cyclone is an anticyclone, and these are generally referred to as highs. The winds around highs rotate in the opposite direction to those in lows.

Both highs and lows tend to drift across the oceans in an easterly direction. Exceptions to this general easterly drift are cyclones that originate in the tropical area located about 25 degrees north or south of the equator. As a cyclone develops and intensifies in this area of the ocean it tends to drift in a *westerly* direction and then start to *recurve*. It starts to recurve to the south and southeast at about 20 degrees latitude in the Southern Hemisphere and north and northeast in the Northern Hemisphere. Exceptions regularly occur to this change in direction in both hemispheres. During the summer cyclone season in either hemisphere, seasoned sailors should be holed up in an area free of the worst of the storms. In the South Pacific, New Zealand and Australia are recommended as good summer destinations (remember that summer south of the equator is winter north of it).

For those wishing to cross the Pacific Ocean to those precious islands where the tradewinds blow and a coconut waits on every tree, there is a time to go and a time to stay. Most cruisers leave the West Coast of the United States in April, May, and June. Common destinations for the first passage are French Polynesia or Hawaii. Most experienced cruisers make their first South Pacific landfall somewhere in French Polynesia. Many sailors recommend traveling to Mexico during the winter months and leaving from there before the Northern Hemisphere summer sets in. This way the Eastern Pacific hurricanes can be avoided. These storm tracks generally tend towards the north and cross the milk-run passage between Mexico and the Marquesas in French Polynesia any time after late May or early June. Cruisers head for specific destinations in the same time frame for good reason; you do not want to be caught in a major blow by making a passage during the hurricane season. [The *coconut milk run* refers to the parade of cruisers heading east across the Pacific from about January to May. As a group, they include West Coast boats and, of course, a sizable contingent that have transited the Panama Canal from the Caribbean and beyond.]

Why is it that we cruisers are always asked if we have ever been afraid at sea or have run into a large storm? No one, it seems, who has not been to sea really wants to hear about the good passages and lazy afternoons lying in a lagoon somewhere exploring an uninhabited atoll. However, ninety-eight percent of the time these are the conditions we have. It seems that all our landlubber friends are more interested in our stories about the two percent of the time that bad weather interrupts our journeys. A gale at sea is enough to ruin your whole day, and you may be fearful for a while. Remember, though, the boat can take most bad weather in stride providing you have prepared for the worst (which rarely comes). People who tell you they have never been afraid at sea are either liars or very foolish—or very lucky that they have never hit bad weather. It can happen: We had one passage from New Zealand to Port Townsend, Washington, which passed without our encountering winds over about 25 knots for the whole distance. We chose the right weather conditions and season for each leg of the journey, which took us thirteen months to complete.

When a big black ugly cloud comes over the horizon, the rule is *reef early*. It is much better to be standing with a yard of sail wrapped around your body in just a little wind than to have all sail up and a 30-knot squall laying you over. With experience, you learn to sort out which squalls are fairly mild and which ones to avoid. If you can see under and through a squall, you can usually take it in stride, plus have a welcome shower in light wind. If a squall covers the whole horizon and is heading your way—reef!

The weather office responsible for a particular area at sea usually forecasts any impending storms. There are many ways to pick up weather forecasts at sea. Amateur radio maritime nets are one of the best means of getting this information. One important facet of the maritime nets is that a storm off to the west (remember the easterly drift) will probably be experienced by another boat before it reaches you, provided you are not first in line. Through the net, you can learn the intensity of the storm, how fast it is moving, and you usually can tell when it will arrive in your area of ocean. (Note that while anyone can listen in on a net, you must have a proper ham license to participate.) Many boats now carry a laptop computer aboard and thus have a means of getting e-mail messages through high-frequency radio from commercial outlets. These suppliers give out a marine weather forecast for their covered areas on a periodic basis. Satellite communication to anywhere in the world is not far in the future for small boats at sea. [The nearly global single-sideband radio system (SSB), which offers weather broadcasts among its many services, is still in business. Rumors of this great system's demise were greatly exaggerated.]

In the South Pacific the New Zealand Met Service provides near-weekly e-mail forecasts through its Auckland office, run by Bob McDavitt (McDavitt's "weathergrams" for sailors appear on the web at www.pangolin.co.nz/yotreps/weathergram.asp and www.bitwrangler.com/yotreps/wxgram). McDavitt has also published an excellent manual that explains in lay terms the terminology used in his weathergrams here, and throughout the South Pacific (*Mariners Met Pack, South Pacific*, available through mcdavitt@met.co.nz for NZ $29.95 plus postage or through

Boat Books, www.webworkshop.com/boatbooks/teach.html, for U.S. $18.40).

What should you watch for when a period of bad weather is heading your way? Most low-pressure systems at sea have associated fronts extending ahead of them. A front sweeps ahead of the low and may be quite active, depending on the low's intensity. A falling barometer and a shift in the wind direction probably mean that the frontal system is approaching. As the front passes, you can expect the wind to increase to an uncomfortable level, rain to fall, the barometer to fall, and seas to rise. The wind continues to shift around until and after the front's passage. Once the front is by, the barometer rises and the wind returns to its normal direction. Depending on how active the front is, this sequence can take anywhere from a few hours to a few days. Regardless, it is best to be reefed down and ready before it reaches you.

Another weather disturbance, the *tropical convergence*, which is similar in action to a front, occurs in areas both north and south of the equator in the tropical zones of the western and mid-Pacific. These slow-moving areas of bad weather develop where the moist warm air of the equatorial zone merges with the cold air of the temperate zones.

A ridge of high pressure usually follows a frontal system. Winds in a very broad ridge are generally light and steady near the center of its associated high. A ridge is an elongated area of high pressure that extends out from a high-pressure cell. An intense high-pressure system makes the tradewinds very boisterous in the area between it and the equator. These tradewinds are referred to as *reinforced trades*. They occur in a *squash zone* directly between the high and the equatorial low, which is a broad trough of low pressure extending roughly along the equator, caused by the heating of the water by the sun. These

Weather

reinforced trades are in the neighborhood of 30 to 35 knots. If a squash zone is predicted for your area, stay put.

* * *

Red at night,
Sailors delight.
Red in the morning,
Sailors take warning.

Just a sailor's ditty, right? No. Scientific analysis has confirmed the validity of this and other long-standing sailors' sayings. What the seamen of old knew from years of weather observation, we can now verify scientifically. Unfortunately, forecasting is still as much art as science, and yesterday's sailors were no better forecasters than today's atmospheric scientists. In my opinion, the ditties are as dependable as anything else.

8

ENGINES AND DINGHIES

Boats are propelled by two methods: wind and engines. I am, of course, aware that oars were, at one time, the only dependable method. However, slaves are hard to find these days so we will limit our discussions to engines. This chapter offers anecdotal experience regarding the selection and use of engines and dinghies that I hope is helpful to the senior cruiser. Maintenance and repair guidance is readily available in other volumes.

ENGINES

First, if you value your boat and life, do not buy any boat with a gasoline-fueled engine for propulsion. I know there are a lot of boats of many sizes that come with "economical" gasoline engines that are "lightweight." We purchased a catamaran a few years ago, and I had to fight with the manufacturer to have small diesel engines put in each hull. Ours was the only boat he built with diesels. "Too heavy," he said. "They will cut your speed down." He was unimpressed when I said that I was not getting the boat for racing, but for cruising. I think the diesel idea caught on, however, because some time later I saw the same cat in our Pacific Northwest powered by a single diesel and outdrive in the center of the boat. Sailboats need the dependability and fuel economy of diesels. When you are clawing off a lee shore or heading into the wind for a safe harbor, you don't have the luxury to blow the engine room for five minutes before you start the motor.

I also advise you to get the biggest motor available within your weight restrictions. It is better to have too much power than too little. Our Westsail 32, GOLDEN BELL, was equipped with a 19-horsepower diesel that was quite adequate for getting in and out of harbor—on a nice day. This concept of just enough is quite satisfactory when all is well. In Greece we were caught by a meltemi, the strong north to northwest wind that blows in the Aegean Sea during the summer months, on a passage to Mykonos. Directly upwind was a fine bay. Our engine would not push the 13-ton boat against the heavy seas. I put up a small sail and motored back and forth through the seas until we finally broke into the shelter of the bay. What could have been a twenty- to thirty-minute run took two hours. An extra 10 horsepower would have made a tranquil day of one that was instead wrought with tension. Had we been young and strong, we could also have spent a couple of hours tacking into the bay, heeling sharply, spray flying, bow bucking. It would have been exciting forty years ago. Have I made a case for plenty of horsepower?

If you are not familiar with diesel engines, take a course in diesel maintenance at your local community college. Ours was taught by a fellow cruiser—not everybody is so fortunate. The instructor began the course with this statement, "Ninety percent of the time the reason your motor doesn't run is because it is not getting any fuel." I fixed our engine several times

80

without doing anything other than blowing out the fuel lines. This process is laborious for an old gaffer like me, so I put an electric pump in the fuel line. What used to take me a half-hour of pumping with the engine's hand pump now takes a few minutes.

Your engine must have clean fuel. If one filter is good, two are better. In GOLDEN BELL we had two filters and one settling basin in the line. We had a serious problem with the tanks. They were black iron, the owner had told us proudly, but they were heavy with flaking, which we didn't know until later. We tried to remove and replace them in Turkey but unfortunately couldn't. Your fuel can also be contaminated at the source. At a marina in St. Thomas in the U.S. Virgin Islands, there was a giant filter in full view to convince us that the fuel was pure. At

The captain must be able to fix the engine, the head, the radio and know how to cook.

the other extreme, in Mexico we were frequently fueled from rusty 50-gallon drums. For protection I had a double-screen filter that I'm sure saved the boat many times.

I don't often cry, but I have shed tears a couple of times replacing the oil filter on our present boat. The filter was positioned deep in the engine compartment and had such little room around it that the usual filter wrench wouldn't work much of the time. As a result I sometimes neglected this onerous task until I could employ a mechanic to do it. Then we had good friends aboard; Don, a retired engineer, suggested an inexpensive kit that allowed us to move the filter from next to the bilge and bolt it to the engine in a completely accessible position. Now, as they say in the shampoo ads, "No more tears!" With clean fuel and clean oil a diesel will serve you well for many years.

When it comes time to purchase an outboard motor, I suggest acquiring the smallest that pushes your dinghy. We currently have an inflatable powered by a 3-horsepower gasoline motor. Yes, gasoline. Where can you find a diesel outboard? Besides, if you keep the motor on deck, it is safe. Before stowing it, turn off the fuel but keep the motor running and let the carburetor run dry. Next, take it aboard, clamp it firmly to a bracket fastened to the boat and padlock and cover it. The bracket should be strong enough so that you don't have to get up in the middle of the night in a raging sea to bring the outboard in for safe keeping. Extra fuel can be carried on deck in a 1-gallon container, pre-mixed and ready to use.

The reason I suggest getting the smallest motor possible is to make it easier to hoist aboard. Most 2-horsepower motors weigh less than 30 pounds. The ultralight motors that weigh in the neighborhood of 8 pounds have little power and won't push very strongly against rough seas or winds. I have had no experience with any of these light motors, however, and suggest you consult with experts. Compromise may be in order; when you are cold, tired, hungry, and anxious to get on board, slow progress can seem an eternity.

DINGHIES

I can only discuss those dinghies I have owned and the reasons I bought them. I have seen every kind, from inboard speedboats on luxury cruisers to a 4-footer in the South Pacific. The 4-footer was owned by a singlehander who brought his under-30-footer engineless sailboat into the Bora-Bora anchorage one day. He was a six-footer himself and looked absolutely ludicrous all doubled up rowing ashore. But he made it in his box with oarlocks.

Our first tender was a 7-foot, hard plastic dinghy with two flotation chambers. With three persons in it, it was nearly awash, but it served us well. It would row easily and rode rough water quite well. It also had a very desirable feature; it fit on the foredeck of our 28-foot GOLDEN FLEECE. Emily loved exploring coral reefs in it; she called it LAMBIE-PIE.

Our second tender was an 8-foot inflatable that could be rolled up and stored aboard. It was very difficult to row, but I felt safe carrying four people in it. Our third, a 12-foot inflatable with a 15-horsepower motor, came with the boat. I could hardly wait to get rid of it and soon did. It was deteriorating rapidly because of the weight of the motor. The original owner wanted to waterski! I replaced it with a hard-bottom Avon inflatable. With the current 3-horsepower motor, we can take four people ashore comfortably.

Once you have a dinghy and engine, you need to figure out a method of getting them aboard quickly and easily. For ocean trips with SUNSET, our Nauticat 38, we hoist the motor aboard using the mizzen sheet, which swings on the mizzen boom out past the stern and has a four-part tackle. We can bring the motor aboard by hand if I am feeling strong and the sea is steady, but the mizzen sheet method is almost too easy to pass up. We use the spinnaker halyard to hoist the dinghy aboard to the fore-deck, where it fits nicely. We recently purchased davits, and the above procedures will soon be history. Davits are a luxury, but don't you deserve a little luxury after working hard all your life? Our davits can be removed by pulling a pin. Incidentally, for open-sea passages, it is not a good idea to keep your dinghy any-where except on deck, where it is preferably stowed upside down unless it is on chocks and covered with a fitted tarp.

9

ELECTRICS: DESIGN FOR SENIORS

By John Strong

When we needed our boat's electrical wiring over-hauled, we decided to turn the job over to real profes-sionals. At that time, John Strong owned a marine electrical service in Portland, Oregon, where we lived. We selected John's firm to do the job, and we couldn't have chosen better. When I told him that I was consid-ering writing this book, he said he'd like to do the chap-ter on electrics: "The industry has advanced so fast and has set standards that are quite tough—and so few know that this has happened." The hope is that this information will help you demand a safe and adequate electrical system for your own boat. —PHK

The first sailboat I owned was little more than a bathtub toy. It was 21 feet long. It was powered by an outboard motor. It had no galley. It had no head. It had no elec-trical system at all. Cruising on that boat was a lot more like camping than cruising. But I was 30 years younger then, and I had a great time in spite of the lack of amenities.

The sailboat I own now is a Victoria 34, an offshore cruising sloop designed by Chuck Paine, built in Southampton, England, and selected by the British Navy as the cadet training yacht. It contains quite a few more conveniences than the bathtub toy. It has refrigeration, an inverter, a microwave oven, all the navigational bells and whistles, an autopilot, forced-air heat, an electric anchor windlass, and a great stereo system. Cruising on this boat is a lot more comfortable, a lot more fun, and a lot more complex.

Every cruising sailor's lifestyle is different. If you can afford to order a new boat from a custom builder, you can get everything you want right from the start. If, however, you buy a new production sailboat, or a used boat, you probably have to make some changes to get the boat to do what you want it to do when you go cruising.

Deciding what you need is the first step. If you've been cruising for years, you have a pretty good idea of what you want on the perfect cruising boat. If you're new to sailing, you probably have lots of ideas based on magazines and boatshows. If you plan to cross oceans, you have a different list of needs than if you intend to cruise close to shore. If you do a lot of coastal cruising, do you like to anchor out, or do you like to stay overnight at marinas and yacht clubs? Will you be using the boat in temperate climates or in the tropics? Will you be cruising for months at a time or just on weekends? Will you be living aboard? Where you go, the length of your cruise, your level of desire for comfort and convenience, and your need for mechanical advantage (equipment to help with the manual labor of sailing and anchoring the boat), all determine what systems you want to include on your perfect cruising boat.

Electrics: Design for Seniors

Getting the systems you want and equipping the boat to support those systems are two separate steps. If two sailboats are equipped the same but one is used for extended cruising away from civilization and the other is used for short cruises and is tied to the dock every night, they need to support their equipment in very different ways. The systems I'm talking about here are the ones that require electric power. The electric power that runs your boat's equipment comes in two varieties: *alternating current*, or AC, and *direct current*, or DC. AC power is what you use at home and when your boat is at the dock, plugged in with that big yellow cord, where it's known as shore power; DC power is what you use in your car, and it comes from batteries.

Let's start with AC power. First, you can't store AC power, unlike DC power. You have to generate it as you need it. If you want to use devices aboard the boat that you normally use at home, you probably need AC power to do the job. In the galley, if you want to use a microwave oven or an electric mixer or a blender, you need AC power. If you use cordless devices powered by batteries, like a shaver, an electric drill, a cellular phone, or a laptop computer, you need AC power for the chargers that charge the batteries.

You basically have three sources for AC power aboard a boat. One is that big yellow cord you plug into the dock, one is a generator, and one is an inverter. The shore power cord is the simplest: plug it in, flip a switch, and there you go. A generator uses an engine to spin an electrical device that makes AC power. The engine that drives the generator uses the same fuel that the boat's main propulsion engine uses; on most modern craft, it's diesel, which is a much safer fuel than gasoline. An inverter makes AC power from the DC power in your batteries. Each source of AC power has its advantages and drawbacks.

The main advantage to that big yellow cord is its simplicity. You can basically use any electrical device or tool that you do at home as long as you don't blow a circuit breaker. The big drawback is that most shore power cords are only 50 feet long. That means you can't get very far from the dock while you're plugged in.

A generator uses fuel, takes up space, makes noise, creates heat and exhaust, and requires maintenance. In some cases, it is the only sensible source for AC power on a cruising boat. If you want an electric stove or air conditioning or hot water from an electric water heater, or even electric heat, you need a generator.

The inverter uses DC power from your batteries to produce AC power. It is quiet, compact, and efficient. It places very large demands on the boat's batteries. Installing an inverter requires some careful planning; batteries and battery charging usually have to be upgraded to support the inverter, especially if you want to use high-demand items like a toaster oven or a hair dryer.

Why can't you use an inverter to run an electric stove or an electric heater? It's a matter of diminishing returns. Most of the devices I mentioned above that need a generator involve what's called resistance heating. Turn it on, and it gets red hot. That takes a lot of energy. (Air conditioning is a form of refrigeration, and refrigeration is a notorious energy sponge.) You can buy an inverter big enough to run any of these devices except the electric stove, but it would take lots of batteries to support that large an inverter. At some point, the weight and size of the batteries would equal that of a generator. And then, how do you charge that many batteries? Answer: with a generator and a battery charger.

To recap, the two sources of AC power you can take with

you cruising are a generator and an inverter. If your boat is less than 45 feet long, it is probably too small for a generator. When you think about it, a 45-foot sailboat probably doesn't have a single unused space as big as a large steamer trunk. That's about how much space a generator takes up. On the other hand, the additional batteries needed to power an inverter can be spread around in smaller spaces.

The batteries on your boat, which start your engine and run your lights and electronics and inverter if you have one, need a source of DC power for charging. If your boat is equipped with an inverter, it probably becomes a battery charger when you are plugged into shore power; most (not all) marine inverters built in the past few years include chargers. If your inverter has a charger, it probably charges just the "house" batteries, not the engine battery. Your boat may have a separate charger that charges your engine battery. If you don't have a generator, all the batteries are charged by the alternator on your engine when you are away from the dock.

The alternator that came with your boat's engine was probably designed to charge a battery big enough to start the engine, and that's about it. It can do a satisfactory job of charging a starting battery, but a poor job of fully charging a large "house" bank of batteries. The rate at which an alternator charges batteries is controlled by a voltage regulator. The internal regulator in most alternators starts to turn the alternator off as soon as the battery voltage starts to rise. Voltage rises rather quickly, long before the batteries are fully charged. So, just as your batteries start to "wake up and pay attention"—that is, accept a charge—the alternator stops charging! This kind of regulation is good enough for a car, where the demands on the battery are light, and it prevents the alternator from working very hard so it will live a long life, but it just isn't aggressive enough to charge a big battery bank in a hurry.

A DC system that truly supports a cruising boat usually requires an upgraded alternator and regulator. The regulator must control the output of the alternator by using a timer in the early stages and then by sensing voltage. Then, when the batteries are fully charged, the alternator must stop charging to keep from damaging the batteries. Therefore, a sophisticated regulator provides a bulk cycle (high output for a fixed length of time) followed by a float cycle (lower output controlled by voltage at the battery) and then turns the alternator off when the batteries are fully charged. Because of these three distinct levels of regulation, these modern microprocessor-controlled devices have become known as "three-step" regulators. They are available from several manufacturers, including Cruising Equipment, Ample Technology, and Balmar, among others.

If you add equipment to your boat, especially an inverter, you probably need to increase the size of the house bank of batteries to support the larger loads. There are choices to be made regarding the type of batteries to use in your boat's cruising system.

The battery in your car is normally what's known as a liquid-electrolyte, or flooded, battery. It's full of electrolyte made of liquid hydrochloric acid, which is nasty stuff. The normal automotive starting battery is vented through little holes in the caps on the top, which allows the battery to breathe as its electrolyte and internal parts warm up and slightly expand when it's being charged. During charging, that nasty acid produces hydrogen gas, which escapes through the vents. More nasty stuff. Remember the *Hindenburg*? It was full of hydrogen gas.

A couple of other types of battery have gained popularity in the cruising community in recent years, and they're sealed, so

90

they won't vent flammable gas under normal circumstances. They use the same basic type of electrolyte, but it's not liquid. One type, known as a gel-cell, uses electrolyte that's in a jellied state. Another uses an absorbent material to hold the electrolyte in suspension, something like a saturated sponge; it's called an absorbed-glass-mat, or AGM, battery.

These new, high-tech batteries are safer because they aren't vented and because they won't spill if they're tipped over. But note that I said they won't vent "under normal circumstances." If something goes wrong with the equipment that charges these sealed batteries and they end up overheating from being overcharged, they release gases under pressure to prevent them from rupturing. Therefore, they should be installed and secured in ventilated compartments just like regular flooded batteries.

The gel-cell and AGM batteries, as well as flooded batteries made for marine house-bank use, are different in another way from batteries used for engine starting. They are called "deep-cycle" batteries because they are built to survive repeated discharging and recharging. That kind of hard use kills regular engine-starting batteries in short order. A common use for deep-cycle batteries ashore is in electric golf carts. In fact, many cruisers whose budgets won't stand gel-cell or AGM batteries (they're quite a bit more expensive than the flooded type) use 6-volt golf cart batteries connected in "series pairs" to produce 12 volts. They're readily available and reasonably priced and offer a lot of bang for the buck.

So, you've determined that your cruising boat needs a larger house bank, comprised of high-quality, deep-cycle batteries. When this bank is discharged, your alternator works especially hard to recharge it because of the bank's size. You definitely need lots of charging capacity if you have gel-cells, because they can accept a higher rate of charge than flooded batteries.

When combined with a larger battery bank that accepts a high rate of charge and a sophisticated voltage regulator that provides that fast charging, the standard alternator that comes with your engine will live a very short life. It simply won't be able to provide enough output without overheating, and it will soon expire. It's not a matter of if; it's a matter of when.

The standard alternator needs to be replaced with a high-output, "hot-rated" unit that can withstand the severe duty of charging a larger number of deep-cycle batteries. When I am cruising under power aboard my sailboat, my high-output alternator gets hotter than my engine's exhaust manifold! In order to survive such heat, it has high-temperature bearings, insulation, brushes, and diodes. And when my alternator is busily pumping 100 amperes into my batteries, it's using about 6 horsepower—almost a quarter of my engine's total output at cruising speed! In fact, after I installed that hefty alternator, I discovered I couldn't reach cruising speed under power when the alternator was working hard. I had to haul the boat and repitch the propeller. As I've so often discovered, in designing systems aboard a complex organism like the modern cruising sailboat, one change begets another. But the system works great. I can spend two days and two nights on the hook and use all the systems, including refrigeration, the biggest single power user on most cruising boats (ah yes, ice cubes!), and fully recharge the batteries in less than 4 hours under way with the engine running.

But even a high-output alternator does not last forever, as I've also learned (the hard way). Consider the analogy of buying new tires for your Porsche: You expect good performance, you expect to pay a healthy price, and you expect the tires to wear out. High-output cruising alternators are the same. They eventually fail. You will burn one up. Carry a spare alternator identical to the one you install on your engine. Carry a complete rebuild kit. When your alternator fails (and it will), you can quickly install the spare and be back in business, and then you can use the kit to rebuild the original when you have time. Come to think of it, carry two rebuild kits. Keep the old original alternator that came with the engine, too—just in case.

So far, in determining your boat's system needs, you have examined your cruising lifestyle and decided on the equipment you need aboard to maintain that lifestyle. You have examined the demands that the required equipment places on your boat's electrical system. You have decided how to upgrade your electrical system to provide enough capacity. And you have figured out how to charge the batteries you need to do the job. Finally, you need some way to measure what is happening when you are charging and when you are discharging. The unit you measure is the "amp-hour."

The ampere is a measure of electrical current. It is easy to determine how many amps a device uses: divide its wattage by its voltage. Consider a light bulb in an interior fixture in your boat; it's a 25-watt, 12-volt bulb. Divide 25 by 12, and what you have is a light bulb that draws about 2 amps. Leave that light bulb burning for 1 hour, and it consumes 2 amp-hours. Simple! The amp-hour is a measurement of electrical usage over time. The capacity of deep-cycle batteries, the type used for your house bank, is measured in amp-hours. Since batteries last much longer if you discharge them only about halfway, you should plan on a house bank that is capable of providing about twice the amp-hours you need between chargings.

In the past few years, several sophisticated system monitors have become available that use a microprocessor to measure current flow and time and to calculate the amount of energy used in amp-hours. They are available from several manufacturers, including Cruising Equipment and Ample Technology. They are programmable, so they know how big your battery bank is, and they tell you to recharge when half of the bank's capacity has been used. Think of these monitors as fuel gauges for your batteries. They tell you how rapidly your alternator is charging your batteries, when they are fully charged, how much load you are presenting to your batteries when you operate your boat's systems, and when your batteries need recharging.

So, your next step is to go back to college and get a degree in electrical engineering, right? Well, no. If you have a basic understanding of electricity and want to tackle designing and installing an electrical system yourself, I suggest you consult some reference material. Two well-worn books on my shelf are *Living on Twelve Volts with Ample Power*, by David Smead and Ruth Ishihara, and *Boatowner's Mechanical and Electrical Manual*, by Nigel Calder. And—this is very important—get copies of sections E-8 and E-9 of *Standards and Recommended Practices for Small Craft*, published by the American Boat & Yacht Council (telephone, 410-956-1050; website, www.abycinc.org). The ABYC book of standards is my bible! If you want to end up with a system that is safe and reliable, be sure all work is done to ABYC standards.

If you prefer to hire a professional to upgrade your vessel's systems, the first step is to make it clear that all work must be done in accordance with ABYC standards. If the electrician you've chosen isn't a member of ABYC, or doesn't know the standard, give him your copies of ABYC E-8 and E-9 for reference. If he doesn't consider the standard important, find another electrician. You spent a lot of money for your boat, and you will spend a lot more getting it ready to go cruising. Don't buy a lot of problems by cutting corners on your electrical system.

Electrics: Design for Seniors

Getting the job done right not only enhances your system's reliability, but its safety. On that subject, let me close with a standard boilerplate recommendation that I include with most of my surveys:

"It is recommended that U/L Listed carbon monoxide (CO) detection devices suitable for marine use be installed in or adjacent to the sleeping spaces aboard your vessel. These CO monitors are to be capable of detecting the presence and the accumulation of CO and alerting persons aboard the vessel by audible and visual means. Open-flame devices such as stoves, fuel-burning heating devices, and all engine exhausts emit carbon monoxide. CO is a colorless, tasteless, odorless gas that combines with red blood cells in the body and inhibits the blood's ability to combine with oxygen. Lack of oxygen to body tissues can ultimately lead to death. Very low concentration levels of CO can progressively poison people. High concentration levels of CO can be lethal in a matter of minutes. Cold, poorly tuned, and overloaded engines produce more CO than warm, properly tuned, and load-matched engines. Gasoline engines produce more CO than diesels, but diesel engines still produce enough CO to cause death because it accumulates in the body over time. Running the engine or generator for battery charging at anchor can produce lethal concentration levels of carbon monoxide. Please refer to American Boat & Yacht Council (ABYC) publication A-24, 'Carbon Monoxide Detection Systems'."

Be prepared, know your systems, be safe, and have fun!

10

MEDICINE FOR GERIATRIC CRUISING

By Mark R. Anderson, M.D.

I met Dr. Mark Anderson when he spoke to our yacht club on accidents, infections, and diseases that were likely to occur to cruisers. Not only were his talk and accompanying handouts well organized, but he was comprehensive, articulate, and easy to understand. Afterwards I asked if he knew geriatrics and if we could some time in the future discuss a book that was germinating in my mind. Since he was a sailor, too, we had an animated discussion during which he agreed to write a chapter oriented toward, but not limited to, the senior cruiser. As an aside, he is constructing a large sailboat in a shed on his property. The hull is uniquely constructed of wood with a method that resembles the cedar-strip construction of many canoes. This will be one strong boat! Some day he will join us cruisers "out there." —PHK

It's certainly true that age can catch up with us in a Murphy's Law affair of multiple things going wrong in shorter and shorter periods of time. Some of these events can be planned for, but many are bolts from the blue. We may know we're at risk, but have no idea when, if ever, we may actually have a problem. So, if you're not already disabled, you're free to go cruising. Deal with what you can; plan for what you can't. If you are disabled, yet still dream of going cruising—well, take the politically correct view that you're differently abled. Work around your problem and go cruising anyway. There are plenty of disabled sailors out there, enough, in fact, that there are programs especially for disabled sailors and designers with experience in accommodating their needs.

Whether we like it or not, various parts of our body deteriorate as we age. What varies are the rates; some deterioriation is responsive to our behavior, and some isn't. We can slow the deterioration of strength by exercise and can do much to maintain our balance by practice. If we start avoiding exposure to loud noises early enough, we can prevent some loss of hearing. We can reduce the chance of cataracts by wearing ultraviolet-blocking sunglasses. Some elderly people are stronger and have better eyesight than many younger people who consider themselves well able to do what they need to do. Know your limitations and work around them.

Unfortunately, as we age, we gradually lose some of our ability to maintain a steady internal chemistry and some of our ability to heal. It's true that ninety percent of our medical problems usually occur in the last ten years of our lives. In younger people it's generally possible to find a single unifying diagnosis to explain any symptoms. In the elderly there may be multiple causes and diseases simultaneously. There may be no unifying diagnosis, which makes it difficult for a physician, or for yourself, to figure out what's wrong with you or your crew out in the middle of the ocean.

You certainly should have a complete medical kit on board. It needs to go far beyond the usual first-aid kit of bandaging materials and over-the-counter medications. You need basic tools, dressing materials, and both over-the-counter and prescription medicines. Remember that all medications have an expiration date. Some may be extended by refrigeration; your pharmacist can perhaps give you such information for specific medicines. It also pays to realize that the label expiration date may only apply to the ideal conditions of an unopened bottle. For example, your nitroglycerin may not expire for a year or so, but the tiny pills lose their potency rapidly upon exposure to air and may be effective for only a matter of weeks once the seal is broken. Include in your kit one or two Foley catheters in case an enlarged prostate leads to urinary retention. Certainly you need a more-than-adequate supply of those medications that you usually take. It is also wise to have a modest supply of prescription medications for problems you hope not to have: antibiotics; cardiac medicine for angina (nitroglycerin); high-blood pressure and heart-failure medications (diuretics and ACE inhibitors); and inhalers such as albuterol in case of wheezing because of infection, asthma, or the onset of emphysema resulting from years of smoking. Don't forget old-fashioned aspirin. An aspirin a day keeps the doctor away by reducing the chance of strokes and heart attacks, aside from its other benefits for pain relief, inflammation reduction, and fever control. Of course, some people just can't take aspirin because of allergy or stomach problems; carry alternatives as well. A very complete suggested kit can be found on my website, www.teleport.com/~andermar.

Keep the kit locked up. Only the captain and first mate

should know where the key is kept. Otherwise, you risk having your kit raided by less well known or trusted crewmembers and then coming up short when you need a medicine most. Keep a log of all medicines and supplies used so you can replenish the kit at your next civilized stop. Note in the log who took what and why. If there's a problem, you may need to justify your actions later. If you are traveling in the third world, you may find it easy to buy medications even without a prescription.

[Dr. Anderson states that only the skipper and first mate should know where the key to the medical chest is kept. I could not agree more strongly based on my experience. I was injured on Nuka Hiva in the Marquesas. I was in great pain and asked my crew (Emily had not yet joined me on the boat), whom I had known for several years and sailed with before, to retrieve my bottle of Tylenol 3 (containing codeine) from the boat. He returned with the bottle; I took two pills and then many more during the night with absolutely no diminution of the pain. I had no relief until I was given a shot of Demerol the next morning. At the next anchorage a doctor warned me that my crew was asking all the boats there for pain pills with codeine. "I think you have a problem," he said. I checked my medicine chest, and of course there were no codeine pills, and some Sudafed tablets were missing. It was then that I realized why I had spent a night of agony on Nuka Hiva. Before the voyage, I had told him not to bring any drugs, and he hadn't. He had just used mine. —PHK]

Next to your kit, your greatest medical asset is your radio. If your radio can reach someone you can be patched through to

100

a physician or other clinician who can help you decide what to do. Near shore a call on VHF 16 may get you assistance within a couple of minutes. This became obvious once when we were relaxing in a quiet anchorage in Barkley Sound, British Columbia. The silence was broken by a frantic call, "Coast Guard, Coast Guard, my son just put sunflower seeds up his nose." A physician was on the radio within a minute to assess the situation and calm the frantic parent. The U.S. Public Health Service can be contacted through the U.S. Coast Guard. A general call to ships in the area with medical staff on board can also bring advice. *Safety and Survival at Sea* by E. C. B. Lee and Kenneth Lee lists the following frequencies for the International Radio Medical Center: 4342 kHz, 6365 kHz, 8685 kHz, 12760 kHz, 12748 kHz, 17105 kHz, and 22525 kHz. Communication is in English, French, and Italian. If you can't contact the center directly, the IRM or other medical help can be reached through the U.S. Coast Guard, RCA, and Globe radio stations of Manila, and the General Pacheco station at Buenos Aires. A ham radio operator's license is another option for long-distance communication. Hams generally go out of their way to connect you with the help you need. Once contact is made, you may be able to handle the situation on board, or can arrange for medical evacuation. Regardless of how you contact help, you need supplies. You need that medical kit.

INJURIES

Anyone can become injured, but with age, injuries occur more easily. Your skin becomes more fragile and heals more slowly. Your bones may become weaker through inactivity. *Osteoporosis* (low-calcium bones) is particularly a problem for post-menopausal women; hormone replacement, calcium supplement, and good physical conditioning helps, but they're not cures.

Everyone falls occasionally and far more often on the unsteady platform of a yacht at sea. Even on land, the average adult falls about twice a year. About seven percent of those falls result in significant injury. On a yacht at sea injury from a fall isn't the only concern. You could fall overboard and be lost. My own experience has taught me how quickly you can fall overboard, even when you are careful.

Why are falls more common in the elderly? There are multiple causes. First are the *musculo-skeletal causes*. We have less strength as we age. Our freedom of movement is reduced because of the pain of arthritis, or our range of motion is limited because the connective tissues of ligaments, tendons, and joint capsules become stiffer with age. Weakness of the legs is a strong correlate of falls. Unfortunately basic exercise isn't all that effective in preventing falls.

In addition, your *balance* may not be what it used to be. Your inner ear's vestibular system may be deteriorating. A stroke, even a minor one from which you thought you had recovered or perhaps never even knew you had, could cause a muscular imbalance that increases your likelihood of falling. Your reflexes to respond to your boat's sudden movements slow down. Even your ability to sense small changes in the position of your extremities can deteriorate.

A whole other category of falls results from your losing consciousness, either completely or partially. Most or all of these events are more common in the elderly. You could have a *seizure* due to brain scarring from a prior stroke, although it's far more likely that a seizure disorder would be previously known. The clue to identifying a seizure is violent shaking, which hopefully someone observes. The victim doesn't remember it, though he or she may remember feeling strange for a short time beforehand. If the victim does remember the shaking, the event was not a seizure. After the shaking stops, there is a period of some minutes before full consciousness returns. There may be loss of bladder control, and the victim may have bitten his or her tongue. Most of the time there is a single seizure and then the return of full function until the next seizure. (Hopefully the next one is prevented through medication, for example Dilantin or phenobarbital.) Multiple seizures without regaining consciousness are more ominous.

You can have sudden loss of consciousness and fall because of a *cardiac rhythm problem*. Cardiac problems are discussed in more detail later in this chapter, but in the context of passing out, the key clue is that there may be no warning. You're feeling fine, and then wham, you're out and on the deck. If the critical rhythm lasts only a few moments you awaken. If not, you've experienced a cardiac arrest. There is no pulse. You do know how to feel for a pulse, don't you? Occasionally you awaken even though the abnormal rhythm continues. Your heart is then pumping well enough to supply the brain when you're supine, but not if you stand. Your crew had better know CPR (cardiopulmonary resuscitation), and you'd better hope you're lucky. Sometimes the bad rhythm is caused by an electrolyte (sodium, potassium, calcium, or magnesium) imbalance, but you have no way of testing for that. Fortunately, electrolyte imbalances are pretty uncommon.

CPR (cardiopulmonary resuscitation) is a very valuable skill that is commonly taught to the public. It saves the lives of many people having cardiac arrests. Unfortunately, its main role is to keep the blood and oxygen flowing for those few minutes until the advanced cardiac life support team can arrive by ambulance and definitive treatment with electric shock and intravenous (IV) medications can be given. CPR by itself saves few lives. Without the availability of advanced care, I think it's more likely to resuscitate a drowning or electrocution victim. Even that's no guarantee.

Passing out a few moments after standing up suggests that your *blood pressure* dropped because your blood stayed down in your feet. This can be due to dilated blood vessels as a reflex after eating, or because of heat or alcohol, or even because of chronic loss of vascular wall tension from chronic disease, such as diabetes. Many medications dilate the blood vessels. Some intentionally have this effect (such as blood-pressure medications and nitroglycerin). The effect is unintentional for other medications, such as the nausea medicine you take for seasickness. If you're somewhat dehydrated, all these causes will be far more likely to make you pass out. Dehydration itself is perhaps the most common of all reasons to pass out soon after standing up. Keep up adequate fluid intake. Have adequate fresh water tankage so you're not rationing your fluids.

Hypoglycemia (low blood sugar) can sometimes occur in the non-diabetic (or pre-diabetic) a couple hours after a large carbohydrate meal. More typically it occurs in the diabetic who didn't eat enough food to match the amount of insulin or oral medication taken. If hypoglycemia is extreme, you pass out, but if your hypoglycemia isn't that severe you just have a rapid heart rate, tremors, and sweating. Unfortunately, some blood-pressure medicines, such as the beta-blockers (propranolol, atenolol, and others), will block these symptoms of the adrenaline your body pours out while trying to raise your blood sugar back to normal. As the sugar drops further, confusion sets in, leading to irrational behavior and ultimately collapse.

Medicine for Geriatric Cruising

Diabetes is increasingly common in the elderly. Diabetes is high blood sugar, (hyperglycemia), but hypoglycemia can occur if your medication (oral or insulin) is excessive for your level of activity and diet. Life at sea can lead to irregular meals and long periods of activity, especially in foul weather. The amount of physical exertion you do at sea may be deceptive. In irregular seas there is almost constant physical activity, even though you've seemingly done nothing productive. If you're diabetic, you've got to be able to monitor your blood sugar regularly and know how to manage your own diabetes far better than most diabetics.

Depression is correlated with falling. I suppose you just don't care enough to maintain attention to the risks of your environment. If you're seriously depressed, I can think of better places to be than out at sea or even in port. Get help.

Fatigue is a great hazard anywhere it's beyond your control. But is it beyond your control? While clawing off a lee shore it might be, but many other times you can heave-to and rest. Are you in a hurry? Some cruisers adopt an attitude of heaving-to very early—for example, if the winds are over 25 knots.

What can we do to prevent falls as a cause of injury and more frequent falls as a consequence of aging processes? Aside from keeping your medical condition tuned up, the obvious steps apply to everyone, regardless of age: pay attention, avoid excessive fatigue, and install plenty of handholds all around your boat, on deck and below. Logically, since increasing weakness with age is such a predictor of the risk of falling, exercise should reduce it. Unfortunately, most exercise doesn't do all that much. However, T'ai Chi Ch'uan, the Asian method involving slow movements emphasizing leg strength and balance through movement and changing postures, does show evidence of benefit. Explore the availability of classes in your locality before you depart.

Typical fractures. Despite all your care and precautions, falls and other injuries occur. You can be seriously injured if you fall from the bosun's chair, are struck by a wild boom, or are thrown across the cockpit or saloon. Certain types of fractures are more typical in the elderly. Other serious internal injuries can occur and be difficult to diagnose.

Hip fractures are quite uncommon except in the elderly. Some physicians believe that the hip may even fracture while you stand or twist, which then causes the fall. Regardless of whether the fall causes the fracture or vice versa, the result is the same. The victim almost certainly can't get up and put weight on the injured leg (though there are the occasional hip fractures in which the bone fragments are compressed together and somewhat stable; that person might bear weight). Typically the pain is obviously in the hip, and when the victim lies down on the back with legs straight out in front, the injured leg is often shorter than the other. Frequently, the leg is also externally rotated—that is, the foot points more to the side. If the examiner lifts the knee slightly while the injured person relaxes, there's pain at the hip. If a light thump with a fist on the heel of the straight leg causes pain at the hip, the hip is virtually certain to be broken. In other words, you can get more useful information without even touching the hip itself. Tenderness over the hip can't clarify whether there's a fracture or just a bruise.

The critical importance of hip fractures is that even if the pieces aren't displaced, there's no good treatment option except surgery to mechanically hold the pieces together and/or replace the hip ball itself with a prosthesis. Sure, if you lie in bed for two or three months the hip will probably heal, and if there's *no* option, that's what you have to do while your crew sails to port. Otherwise, you'd better use your radio and arrange your evacuation because a major risk of prolonged bed rest is developing *deep-vein thrombophlebitis (DVT)*. These blood clots can then break off and be carried to your lungs and kill you. Called pulmonary emboli, if they don't kill you immediately, they are felt as sudden shortness of breath, followed by painful breathing. Minor cases can be difficult to diagnose.

Wrist fractures occur at all ages, but incidences peak when people are in their sixties. They're usually caused by a fall onto the outstretched palm. There'll be bony tenderness at the wrist. If there's significant displacement, it'll often be seen as a "silver fork" deformity—the wrist takes a bend up (away from the palm). Displacement simply means that the bone pieces aren't aligned as they're supposed to be. If there's visible deformity, you can be sure that the fracture should be reduced—that is, "set." Often there is enough displacement seen on x-rays to indicate a need for reduction, even if it isn't visible externally. It seems that around half of all wrist fractures should be reduced. Assuming there's good blood flow to the fingers and no true numbness, reduction can be delayed for up to seven to ten days if need be. If the bones heal out of place, there'll be more disability, but at least it's not life threatening. Certainly the wrist, and any other limb fracture, should be splinted. Splint materials should be in your medical kit, or you can make do with a well-padded board and an elastic wrap. Inflatable splints are an easy temporary measure but aren't as versatile or durable as having rolls of fiberglass splint material that only needs wetting and wringing out before applying it to the limb over some padding.

Here's as good a place as any to debunk a myth. Even though a bone is broken, you usually can still move it, though

107

doing so hurts. The key findings of fractures are: (1) bony point tenderness (not just tenderness of the overlying soft tissues), (2) loss of function (you can't use it normally), (3) deformity, and (4) crepitation—that is, grating of the bone ends with movement. The first two characteristics are virtually universal. The last two are less frequent. If you get pain at the injured area when the bones or joints are stressed, there's either a fracture or sprain. So if you grasp the limb and tweak it a bit without touching the painful area, you get more useful information than by just touching the sore area directly.

Shoulder fractures are also more common as you age. The shoulder is a shallow ball-and-socket joint with the head of the humerus, the upper arm bone, being the ball. Often the head of the humerus is broken off. Any minimal movement is very painful, and usually there is quite dramatic swelling, followed by bruising, that develops over the shoulder. There's usually no easily visible deformity. Surgery is rarely done in the elderly, and the treatment is just placing the arm in a sling, preferably with a strap to hold the upper arm against the body.

Rib fractures are common after falling against something or landing with the arm between the chest and ground or deck. It hurts to breathe. Squeezing the chest between spine and breastbone, or from side to side, causes pain that is well localized to the fracture. If you push on one rib at a time, you find one or more that clearly trigger the pain at the fracture, even if you're pushing several inches away from the fracture. Chest wall injuries without fracture, for example cartilage injuries, don't generally have this last finding. Rib fractures can even occur just because of forceful coughing or sneezing when the bones are weak. It's certainly a case of "it hurts to laugh."

It usually doesn't matter whether there's a rib fracture or not, except in a couple of cases. If several adjacent ribs are bro-

108

ken in multiple places you may see a section of chest between the fractures suck in as the victim inhales. This "paradoxical" movement means that this lung can't be ventilated very well. A much more serious injury, it is called a flail chest. The immediate first aid is to lie with the injured side down against a cushion. Evacuation should be arranged. Fortunately this condition is quite uncommon.

Otherwise, rib fractures are just a matter of relieving the pain adequately for a few weeks, unless there's a punctured or badly bruised lung. Lung problems show up as increasing shortness of breath, as opposed to it just hurting to breathe. There may be bloody sputum. On rare occasions, a lung is punctured, and the air getting outside the collapsing lung builds up increasing pressure. Called *tension pneumothorax*, this goes on to push the heart way over to one side so that the aorta gets kinked off. Shock develops, along with extreme shortness of breath. The injured side of the chest gets visibly overinflated, and the windpipe, felt in the notch at the top of the breastbone, is pulled to the side opposite the injury. Tapping on the overinflated side of the chest sounds more drumlike than on the opposite side. Death follows rapidly. The life-saving move, while you're calling for evacuation, is to put a large needle through the chest a couple inches below the collarbone to deflate the pressurized overinflated side. Please don't do this procedure unless you're sure you're not misreading the situation and that otherwise the victim is dying. Fortunately, tension pneumothorax is rare.

Crushing of individual vertebrae in the spine is quite common, particularly from a fall landing on the buttocks or in a standing position with the force transmitted up to the spine. Particularly in women with osteoporosis, these *vertebral compression fractures* can occur spontaneously. It hurts to move the spine, but there is no obvious deformity. It may be tender directly over the collapsed portion of the spine. Numbness, paralysis, and nerve damage are extremely rare. In the day or so after the injury the belly may become bloated because the gut may take a holiday and not move things along. This is usually treated by resting the gut with IV fluids, but you may get by with a liquid diet if there's not too much vomiting. Otherwise, treatment is again just a matter of pain relief and staying in bed most of the time for several days.

Head injuries. Head injuries can occur at any age, but our more fragile vessels as we age may make brain injury more common. Suppose you're in the middle of the ocean. Someone has a head injury, perhaps from an uncontrolled gybe, and is knocked out. If that person awakens within a couple minutes and then continues to improve, you can be reasonably comfortable just watching the victim. Headache, per se, isn't a good predictor of serious injury. On the other hand, if that person starts deteriorating—that is, shows increasing confusion, repetitive persistent vomiting, clumsiness, or weakness of part of the body, you'd better worry and arrange an evacuation. Just being knocked out or severely dazed is a concussion. There is no visible brain injury. Worsening implies that bleeding or swelling within the skull may be compressing the brain. That's a problem that needs accurate diagnosis and possibly surgery.

Intra-abdominal injuries. Injuries to internal organs in the belly are tricky to diagnose without advanced procedures and high technology. Seek guidance if there's significant traumatic abdominal pain. The two abdominal organs most frequently seriously injured are the spleen and liver. They're on opposite sides of the abdomen under the low ribs. If either area is very tender after a fall and you can't be sure it's just a superficial bruise, you should be worried. Try to separate rib tenderness from abdominal tenderness. Internal bleeding can occur fairly silently. If the victim gets lightheaded and has a rapid pulse (over 120 beats per minute) when he or she stands up, you really ought to be worried. Organize that evacuation.

ARTHRITIS

Enough of this morbidly alarming talk. Such injuries are mercifully unlikely. Arthritis is not. It's usually just another consequence of gravity gradually winning. Our bearings, our joints, eventually wear out. Although your aching knee might help you forecast that approaching low-pressure system, what will you do about the pain in the meantime? Keep warm, keep mobile, and be careful. The standard medications are the nonsteroidal anti-inflammatories such as aspirin, ibuprofen, ketoprofen, naproxen, and a host of prescription-strength pills of the same and other medications. The key to inflammation control is taking adequate dosages for an adequate time. The occasional low dose relieves some pain and controls a fever, but inflammation requires more. High doses are needed, and they need to be taken consistently; the anti-inflammatory effect doesn't kick in for three to five days. In the case of ibuprofen, for example, this means taking 600 to 800 mg. three times a day. That's nine to twelve over-the-counter-strength pills daily.

Unfortunately, there's very real risk with a consumption level this high. The most common problem is stomach upset, which can lead to ulcers and bleeding. Taking the pills with food helps. So does taking them with antacids and medicines

111

that reduce stomach acid secretion. These are discussed under abdominal problems later in the chapter. Intestinal bleeding can be seen as passing stools that are black like tar. The bleeding can be slow and hidden or catastrophically fast.

The other problem with taking anti-inflammatory medications is that chronic use can cause kidney damage, and that's definitely more likely in the elderly. Chronic use can also cause liver damage, not to mention other possibilities. Nothing's perfect; these medications are great, but there's risk with everything.

SENSORY PROBLEMS

Some of our senses may become less acute with age. There is typically a loss of hearing, especially of the higher frequencies. Hearing loss is accelerated by excessive noise. Too bad you can't reverse that hearing loss caused by noise you heard decades ago. Cataracts are far more likely with age. We've learned that ultraviolet light exposure is one of the major causes. That's why it's so important to have sunglasses that block UV light. Unfortunately, the damage is cumulative, so you may have received your damaging UV years ago. Vision deteriorates in one or both eyes. Halos may appear around lights at night. Fortunately, surgery can remove cataracts, and today's prosthetic lenses are far better than the extremely thick glasses of old. Unfortunately, you can't focus a plastic lens the way you can a natural one.

Loss of hearing and sight can have a significant effect on navigation and safety if you can't hear foghorns, buoys, and breakers or can't see well enough to read the chart, follow a compass course, or spot that buoy or landmark. Have your hearing checked before you leave. Get an appropriate hearing aid and mention your needs regarding weather exposure. Once out cruising, keep a very active lookout. Correct your vision as much as possible. Radial or laser keratotomy is on option for some but often doesn't remove the need to wear glasses. Your eye's lens gets stiffer as you age so you develop difficulty changing its focus. This is why close-up work gets more difficult. Use binoculars, good lighting at the chart table, and magnifying lenses. The magnifiers that you wear like glasses free your hands for chartwork.

MENTAL ACUITY

The benign forgetfulness of aging can also present hazards. Making notes of courses, landmarks, and waypoints may be helpful. Stowage lists are handy whatever your age. Dementia is more severe and progressive and is often unnoticed or denied by those developing it. Hopefully, the partner sees this condition developing and either can work around it, taking more of the load, or know when it's time to call it quits.

ENVIRONMENTAL HAZARDS

Our bodies gradually lose some ability to maintain a steady body temperature. Tropical environmental stresses can aggravate this. Sweat production decreases with age. It also decreases with many medications, especially those used for seasickness, allergy, and nausea. Heat exhaustion develops more easily and can progress to heat stroke. Heat stroke involves total loss of temperature control, the loss of sweating, and high fever. Hot dry skin with a fever over 104° Fahrenheit is the rule. Rapid cooling is mandatory. Place the victim in the shade and put ice bags under the arms and in the crotch. Continuously wet his or her skin with cool water and fan the body to promote evaporation. The lesser problem of heat exhaustion responds to oral fluids, rest, and shade.

INTERNAL MEDICINE DISORDERS

It's clearly impossible to cover the entire scope of medicine in one chapter. The discussion here briefly summarizes a number of acute medical problems that more typically occur in the elderly, although they can occur at any age. If you use this section to make a tentative diagnosis of yourself, please pay close attention to my choice of words.

Cancer. In a discussion of cancer and cruising, prevention and detection are the main issues. Reasons to seek evaluation at the end of a passage include substantial unexplained weight loss, night sweats, chronic cough or hoarseness, coughing up blood, blood in stools, wounds that won't heal, and enlarging or changing skin lesions. Prostate screening by digital rectal exam and PSA testing are important for men, as are breast self-exam and pap smears for women.

Skin cancer is usually caused by cumulative UV light damage. Use a sunscreen. There are three types of skin cancer. Two skin cancers, squamous cell and basal cell, are easy to cure. Malignant melanoma, on the other hand, is often fatal. Especially if you're fair skinned and burn easily, pay close attention to all your existing skin lesions so that you'll notice any new ones or any change in old ones. Close photographs of your back, to record those you can't personally see, help to document any change.

Heart problems. *High-blood pressure*, or hypertension, is a silent killer as it causes slow damage. Usually there are no symptoms. Getting it under control before you leave and knowing your medications is important.

Atrial fibrillation (AF) is a fairly common abnormal rhythm that can develop any time and from many causes. Know how to feel and count your pulse. Although a normal pulse rate varies over time, from beat to beat it should be quite regular. Atrial fibrillation occurs when the upper chamber of the heart stops setting a regular beat. It's felt as an irregularly irregular pulse—that is, there's no pattern in its rhythm. Many people can tell the change the instant it starts, but some can't. Often the rate is quite fast, 120 to 150 beats per minute or more, when it starts and isn't treated. This rate puts an extra load on the heart and can cause pain, trouble breathing, and dizziness. If the rate is less than 100, it's usually well tolerated but still not a rhythm you want to stay in if you can avoid it. Prompt medical attention or radio guidance of onboard treatment may convert you to a regular rhythm. It can also end all by itself. Digoxin (Lanoxin) and diltiazem (Cardizem) are two medications commonly prescribed to reduce the heart rate to a tolerable level and possibly even convert the rhythm back to normal. The risk of staying in atrial fibrillation more than several days is that a blood clot can form in the heart and then break off and cause a devastating stroke. To prevent this possibility, the blood should be thinned with an aspirin a day or with stronger medications.

Paroxysmal supraventricular tachycardia (PSVT) is another sudden rapid rhythm. Instantaneously the heart rate jumps to 150 per minute or more. It ends just as instantaneously, but can last from seconds to hours. It differs from AF in that, although fast, the pulse is absolutely regular. You may be able to get it to stop by vagal maneuvers such as holding your breath and plunging your face into a pan of ice water or covering it with a cold wet cloth. Or do the *val salva* maneuver: Hold a deep breath while bearing down and straining as if you're constipated or trying to push out a baby. Carotid massage carries a risk of stroke if there's atherosclerosis, but can be effective in aborting PSVT. It's done by vigorously massaging one side of the neck under the jaw at the carotid pulse. Medications that you might be carrying, such as beta-blockers, can also stop the rhythm after they're absorbed.

When part of the heart muscle doesn't get enough blood flow, *myocardial ischemia* develops. If temporary, this condition causes *angina pectoris*, heart pain without permanent damage. If the blood flow is stopped, as by a clot forming where there was previously just a constriction, a *heart attack*, or myocardial infarction, occurs.

Here's a brief description of "typical" heart pain. It's a pressure, a squeezing or dull ache felt in the center of the chest (not to the left over the heart) that is usually brought on with exertion and relieved by rest. Often the individual does not call it a pain and may demonstrate it by holding a fist over his or her breastbone. The pressure may radiate to the neck, teeth, arms, back, or occasionally, the upper mid-abdomen. It may only appear in those places. The association with exertion, fright, anger or after eating a meal is important. These all increase the work of the heart. Pain triggered by exertion is the most suspicious. Untreated angina (pain without damage) lasts less than 15 to 30 minutes (assuming you stop and rest). The more the pain is associated with nausea, vomiting, shortness of breath, cold sweats, dizziness, or palpitations and the longer it lasts (more than 30 to 60 minutes), the more likely it is that it has progressed to a heart attack with damage and/or death of heart muscle. Sometimes, particularly in women, the elderly, and diabetics, there may be no pain but just the other associated

116

symptoms or a sense of overwhelming weakness. Several other things may precisely mimic, or be mimicked by, heart pain. Esophageal pain or an ulcer is probably the most common mimic, but also consider acute lung problems (some potentially fatal), rupturing or dissecting aneurysm (highly lethal), gall bladder attack, pericarditis (inflammation of the sack around the heart), and other causes.

This description should give you a good idea of what to worry about. If symptoms develop, rest first. Take an aspirin because it inhibits clot formation. (In fact, you should probably be taking an aspirin a day for prevention.) If you have nitroglycerin aboard, take a tablet under your tongue. Assuming the symptoms are new, you should get to a hospital for a more complete evaluation or get on the radio to seek further advice. If you've had angina before and this attack is the same as previous episodes, there's less immediate concern. However, if angina is changing, becoming more frequent or severe, it's considered unstable and threatening to progress to a heart attack. Anyone with a history of angina needs to get this condition well under control before departing on any trip.

Congestive heart failure (CHF), if new, is often triggered by a heart attack that may be "silent." Otherwise, it is a failure of the heart to pump as much blood as is demanded of it, and the blood backs up. Typical symptoms include abnormal shortness of breath with exertion, worsening breathing if lying down so there's a desire to sleep seated or propped up on a few pillows, waking up at night short of breath, getting up at night to urinate more than once, and as both sides of the heart progressively fail, swelling in the legs. Sudden severe attacks can occur that produce extreme trouble breathing. If you listen to the lungs, the breath sounds are probably filled with wet crackling sounds. The victim wants to sit bolt upright, and there may be

117

pink frothy sputum. Death follows without rapid intervention. Nitroglycerin and potent water pills (diuretics like furosemide [Lasix]) are key.

Perhaps the most common problem confused with angina is *gastroesophageal reflux disease (GERD)*. Basically, this is heartburn, pain caused by stomach acid getting into the food pipe. How can you distinguish esophageal pain from angina? Ultimately you can't with certainty, but there are clues that give some reassurance that you're experiencing esophageal pain. It's not typically triggered by exertion, although position may cause it. Leaning over or lying down may cause stomach acid to flow into the esophagus. It may occur after a large or spicy meal. Look for clues such as a burning pain, belching, regurgitation, or a bitter taste in the mouth. The pain may last many hours without change. Heart pain generally doesn't last continually for many hours but may come and go over many hours. Esophageal pain won't cause true difficulty breathing. It may be relieved quickly with liquid antacids such as Maalox or Mylanta. More lasting relief can result from suppressing stomach acid with medications such as Pepcid or Zantac. Prevention is by not overfilling the stomach and by sleeping with the head somewhat elevated.

Esophageal spasm is a cramp of the esophagus that really can feel identical to heart pain but still isn't exertional and may last much longer and without true difficulty breathing. It won't be relieved very well by antacids, but nitroglycerin may work by relaxing the muscles. Sometimes just drinking very hot water helps.

Disaster can strike when the aorta, the large artery leading from the heart, suddenly starts to rip between the layers of its wall. This *aortic dissection*, which fortunately is rather rare, generally occurs in those with a long history of high-blood

118

pressure. It frequently strikes as a severe sudden tearing pain in the chest. It may be described as like "being hit by a baseball bat" and commonly is also felt in the back. It may spread out from the chest up into the neck and down the arms and into the abdomen. The back component is an important clue. Rapid medical attention is mandatory, and surgery is frequently needed. Time is of the essence.

Lung problems. I've already touched on chest trauma. Now I'll touch on lung problems. *Asthma* and *emphysema* can be considered together. Emphysema usually develops after more than twenty years of smoking. Asthma may be present from childhood. Both are characterized by wheezing, a whistling sound in the lungs heard with exhalation. The sound is caused by a narrowing of the smaller airways of the lungs. The treatable component of this narrowing is due to the tiny muscles in the walls of the airways tightening down. That bronchospasm is reversible. You'd think that sufferers would be aware they had these problems, but many deny them and may only admit to a chronic cough. When something, such as dust, allergy, or infection, causes a flare-up of emphysema or asthma, acute shortness of breath develops. Wheezes become more obvious to the bystander or can be detected by putting an ear or stethoscope to the chest. If the bronchospasm is severe, wheezes may disappear, breath sounds become faint, and more apparent is a long expiratory phase of breathing, lasting more than 3 seconds.

Simplistically speaking, the treatment of wheezing is with inhalers such as albuterol (Ventolin and Proventil) for the bronchospasm and anti-inflammatory steroids such as prednisone. Seek guidance. Antibiotics help only if there is a bacterial infection, such as is suggested by fever and lots of yellow or green sputum.

Pneumonia and *bronchitis*, although they can have non-infectious causes, are generally lung infections resulting from either bacteria or viruses. The difference is that bronchitis is an infection of the airways of the lungs, and pneumonia involves the lung tissue itself. Both have cough. Either can have fever. Well-established pneumonia may develop rattling breath sounds, true shortness of breath, and painful breathing on one side of the chest. Colored sputum and high fever make a bacterial cause more likely. Have appropriate antibiotics on board to treat the bacterial forms.

Abdominal problems. *Peptic* disorders are all caused by stomach acid. They include GERD (discussed under chest pains earlier) plus *ulcers* and *gastritis*. Remember that GERD is commonly called heartburn and is felt in the middle of the chest. Eating smaller meals and sleeping with the head elevated reduces the reflux of acid up into the esophagus. Typical ulcers are felt as very well localized pain and tenderness in the middle of the upper abdomen. You can often point at ulcer pain with one finger. Ulcer pain is often like a bad hunger pang. It may be briefly relieved by food but then returns. Gastritis pain is similar. Aggravating factors for all the peptic disorders are anti-inflammatory medications like aspirin and ibuprofen, plus alcohol, smoking, and caffeine. Treat peptic problems with antacids and medications that reduce acid secretion such as Pepcid, Axid, Zantac, or Tagamet. To get their full effect requires four pills a day. Prilosec is a more potent medicine, but it's only available by prescription. Some ulcers are associated with an infection, but you'd have no way of knowing that so don't take antibiotics without medical guidance. Watch for those black stools that indicate bleeding, and consider less obvious bleeding if there is progressive weakness developing over days or weeks. If there's a dramatic increase in ulcer pain followed by diffuse abdominal pain, tenderness, and a boardlike rigid abdomen, the ulcer may have perforated, and you need surgery.

Anyone can get *gastroenteritis (GE)*, and traveling makes it common. Commonly called a stomach flu, the primary symptoms are vomiting and diarrhea. Food poisoning is a form of gastroenteritis. Abdominal pain is fairly minor or crampy and not localized, and there's little tenderness. The majority of cases, whether viral or bacterial, are self limited. Treatment consists of stomach rest by clear liquids for a day or so, prevention of dehydration by frequently drinking small amounts, and taking pills or suppositories for nausea or vomiting if necessary. If there's a lot of cramping, a high fever, and especially bloody diarrhea, the probability of bacterial or parasitic cause goes up. Even bacterial GE may run its course without antibiotics, but antibiotics can often shorten the course and be more necessary in the elderly to reduce complications. Parasitic infections require specialized antibiotics and lab tests for diagnosis.

Constipation is commonly caused by insufficient activity, insufficient fluids, and a diet lacking in roughage. There is certainly a place for laxatives and stool softeners, but recognizing the cause and responding accordingly is more important. Remember that there is no rule saying you need a bowel movement daily. That's a bit of old-time medical misinformation and advertising propaganda.

Constipation becomes serious, however, when it's part of a *bowel obstruction*. This condition develops over a few days. First, there's no passage of stool and then no passage of gas. The belly distends with gas, and abdominal cramps develop. Since the normal way out is blocked, your body decides to

121

reverse course. Vomiting starts, first with stomach contents, then with yellow bile, followed by green bile; then comes increasingly brown and foul vomit until you're bringing up liquid stool. Although there is usually lots of crampy pain, the belly is generally not very tender. Since you can't eat during this condition, you get dehydrated. The usual treatment is bowel rest (that is, nothing by mouth), IV fluids, and surgery. If it's a partial obstruction, surgery may be avoided. Since the common causes of obstruction are scarring from previous surgeries, a hernia that slides out and gets stuck, and tumors, obstructions are more common as you age. The corollary is that your risk is much less if you've never had abdominal surgery and you don't have a hernia.

Diverticuli are tiny pouches that develop in the walls of the large bowel, usually after the age of fifty-five. People who consume more roughage in their diet are less likely to develop them. Once you have them, they don't go away. You are unaware of their existence until they develop problems. They can bleed, in small or large amounts. Since the bleeding is close to the anus, it is bright red or burgundy colored. Bleeding from the stomach and small intestine shows as black stool due to digestion of the blood, unless the bleeding is very rapid in which case the stool may be burgundy colored and especially foul smelling. *Diverticulitis* is an infection of the diverticuli and is felt as pain and tenderness in the lower left quarter of the abdomen, with or without fever. It can usually be treated by oral antibiotics unless severe. Severe diverticulitis, with high fever, can progress to a perforation of the bowel. Then the abdomen becomes hard and extremely tender to the touch, with this feeling spreading over the entire abdomen. Perforation requires surgery.

You can think of *appendicitis* as somewhat comparable to

122

diverticulitis but in the lower right quarter of the abdomen. It can mimic many other things, but any abdominal pain with tenderness in the lower right part of the abdomen should be considered possible appendicitis first, and help should be sought. Almost invariably there is a loss of appetite, and the symptoms generally develop over a day or so.

Sudden severe steady abdominal or back pain, without injury or strain, may mean a rupturing abdominal *aortic aneurysm*. The loss of pulses in the groin is strong, though inconsistent, evidence. Collapse and shock can be rapid. A rupturing aneurysm is a surgical emergency. Time is of the essence.

Genitourinary problems. In post-menopausal women, any vaginal bleeding must be considered cancer until proven otherwise.

Urinary tract infections (UTI) are common in the elderly and may show no localizing signs, just a fever. Typical symptoms are painful, frequent, and hesitant urination with a sense of urgency. Adequate fluid intake decreases the likelihood of UTIs. If fever and back pain develop, especially with tenderness over a kidney (in the back to one side just below the ribs), consider the more serious progression to *pyelonephritis*, a kidney infection. Kidney infections are more likely to need intravenous antibiotics. Urine test strips can detect *leukocytes*, white blood cells, in UTIs.

Urinary infections in older men usually result from difficulty emptying the bladder due to enlargement of the prostate gland. Older men should be screened for prostate cancer, but the more common problem is *benign prostatic hypertrophy (BPH)*, or enlargement. This condition develops slowly as diminished urinary stream, hesitancy, and needing to void more frequently, demonstrated by getting up more than once during the night to urinate. The side effects of medications (especially antihistamines and nausea medications) or infection can be the last straw leading to *urinary retention*, the total inability to pass urine. The man knows that he's feeling uncomfortably full and can't empty his bladder. There are many types of catheters, but the Foley type is most common and generally used. These catheters have an inflatable balloon near the end that can be filled with air or water to prevent the catheter from falling out. Also carry disinfectant and lubricant so that the catheter can be passed to relieve the obstruction. Your physician can instruct you in passing a catheter, or you can get radio guidance. After relieving the obstruction, the catheter can be removed, but the obstruction may return. If it does, you need to pass a catheter again and leave it in. In any event, consider an episode of urinary retention as an indication that urological evaluation of the need for definitive surgery is called for.

Perhaps the worst pain commonly experienced is that due to *kidney stones*, or urolithiasis. Although occasionally the pain may be mild, more typically it strikes as a severe cramp or steady pain in one flank, progressing down and around toward the groin. The sufferer can't find a position of comfort and frequently is very restless, pacing back and forth. He or she may break out into a sweat and start vomiting. A urine test strip almost always detects blood, but it may not be enough to be visible to the naked eye. Unless the condition is complicated by infection, treatment is drinking lots of fluids and taking strong narcotic pain pills. A non-narcotic anti-inflammatory pain pill, Toradol, is adequate in some cases. It may take hours or days to pass the stone. When the stone passes into the bladder the pain subsides. Large stones may not pass without surgical assistance.

Kidney stones become life threatening, rather than just painful, when infection develops in the blocked kidney. More tenderness in the flank develops, along with fever. Oral antibiotics may temporize but are not usually enough. The blockage needs to be relieved. Get help.

Neurological problems. When a part of the brain gets insufficient blood, localized neurological symptoms develop. The symptoms can be virtually anything, but common ones are difficulty speaking or swallowing and one-sided weakness, paralysis, or numbness. If the symptoms resolve within 24 hours, you have experienced a *transient ischemic attack (TIA)*. If the symptoms persist, you've had a *stroke*, meaning some permanent damage to the brain, although some recovery is the rule if the stroke doesn't kill. Most strokes are caused by blood clots, although about ten percent, usually those with prominent headache, are caused by bleeding. Stroke is such an apt name, isn't it? Since aspirin has a blood-thinning effect, a single aspirin a day can reduce the chance of strokes just as it does for heart attacks. Unfortunately, for all practical purposes, there's no treatment of strokes except supportive care and rehabilitative therapy.

Seizures are basically an electrical short circuit in the brain so that most or all of the brain fires off simultaneously. Brain scarring from previous injury or stroke is a possible cause for new seizures in the older patient. Almost always the victim loses consciousness and has no memory of what happens. Usually the entire body stiffens for some seconds and then shakes vigorously for a minute or two. Then comes several minutes of lethargy and confusion before full clear-headed consciousness returns. The victim may have a bitten tongue and soiled clothes. During a seizure bystanders should do nothing except to protect the victim from injury or falling overboard. If it's the first seizure, it may not ever happen again, if you're lucky. If it's a known seizure disorder give an extra dose of medication. Unless multiple seizures develop, usually further evaluation can wait until you reach land, though close observation is warranted.

Diabetes and alcoholism are two common causes of *peripheral neuropathy*, which is the slow development of numbness in the extremities. It usually involves both feet and spreads over months or years. If you have or develop it, you have more difficulty knowing where your feet are, so you are more likely to fall. You don't feel the early signs of cold injury. If the numbness is more localized and accompanied by back or neck pain, consider a ruptured disk.

Poor blood circulation to the legs usually develops slowly. Hardening of the arteries is the usual cause, and it's more accelerated in diabetics, smokers, and those with high blood pressure. An early sign is the loss of your toe hair. Your feet become more prone to cold. A calf pain that occurs with walking is called *claudication* and is analogous to heart angina. Aspirin may help, but you should seek medical attention in port.

Both neuropathy and circulatory problems make you more prone to exposure injury to the extremities—cold nip, frostbite, and chronic immersion injury. Keep those feet and hands warm and dry.

I've made no attempt to make this discussion of medical issues all inclusive. I've tried to touch on the more common and/or significant emergency disorders, particularly those that occur more typically as we age. I hope I've presented enough information so that you're aware of the scope of the problem, but I hope I haven't scared you away from your dream.

Be prepared. Be knowledgeable. Have fun.

11

THE SAILING LADY

By Emily Tufts Keller

T he cruising life is a new adventure for most of us, even
if we have been daysailing or on short cruises in past
years. Closing the house, putting belongings in storage,
and heading out with no set time to return and no definite
itinerary is scary. A cruiser is a vagabond, at one with the sea
and waterways, the sky and stars, wild creatures, other peoples
and other cultures. Whether a woman sets out on a prolonged
voyage as skipper on her own boat or in partnership with a
husband or significant other, she must be self-reliant, adaptable, inquisitive, prepared, and willing to give up a comfortable
life for the unknown. As familiar landmarks disappear astern,
the worries and concerns of land-based life drop away; a
cruiser begins to look forward, alert to what lies ahead.

Life aboard a cruising sailboat involves the same domestic responsibilities as shoreside but under more primitive and cramped
circumstances. Cruising boats vary widely in such amenities as
refrigeration, freezers, stoves with ovens, microwaves, hot and

cold running water, and most of all space. Whatever your boat has or does not have, there are meals to prepare, clothes to wash, and surfaces to tidy and clean. Lack of luxuries means greater ingenuity in shipboard life.

As the years take their toll we lose strength and balance, we may have special nutritional or medical needs, and we find that wounds do not heal as well as they used to and that our vision and hearing may be diminished—we just plain aren't as tough as we were. On the plus side, I like to hope we have gained wisdom and can recognize our strengths and weaknesses.

Before leaving on an extended cruise you should have a medical evaluation to provide management advice on any present medical problems as well as general advice to maintain health. A person receiving long-term medication for diabetes or asthma or for heart, blood pressure, kidney, or other conditions should arrange to procure an adequate supply to last the duration of the trip or to refill recurring prescriptions along the way. An arrangement for communicating with the primary-care physician in case of trouble would also be wise.

Osteoporosis, or diminished bone density, can predispose you to fractures, particularly if you are a post-menopausal woman with a light frame. Your doctor may suggest diet changes or hormone replacement. In any event, exercise, particularly weight-bearing exercise, is important in maintaining bone density, strength, and agility. No matter how large or luxurious your boat is, there is no space aboard for a nice walk. Long passages need to be broken by periods at anchor to allow for trips ashore to walk, shop, and explore. Rolling along down the tradewinds requires constant need to hold on, and here is where well-placed handholds throughout the boat are helpful for the balance-challenged. The constant use of muscle for preparing a meal in a plunging boat, holding on to sit, and even being tossed about in the bunk is tiring, but not the type of exercise needed for maintenance of bone calcium.

Fortunately, shopping for supplies in the various villages and cities you visit usually involves a nice walk. Shopping was one of my greatest pleasures in the cruising life. Keeping the larder stocked means a trip ashore, which in other countries is an introduction to the local community life. In Spain we were in a marina several miles east of Sitges. The path to town led along cliffs carpeted with rosemary, which provided a twig or two to flavor the next meal. (It also led along a topless beach— the captain, of course, went along to help carry packages.)

Emily's highlight of the week—going to the Friday market in Kusadasi, Turkey, and finding vegetables fresh from the farm.

Visiting the market, the laundry, the post office, and the bank allows you to experience local life. While cruising in Europe I developed foraging techniques. The bakery was easy. A few sniffs of the morning air soon located the odor of fresh-baked bread. Noting where people with bags of groceries had just come from allowed me to find the source—the grocery store. Finding the laundry was harder, because I needed to ask someone and then understand the answer. Most people were interested and helpful. We tried local cuisine as much as possible, but peanut butter withdrawal was serious. Once a grocery clerk trying to understand my question suddenly brightened and said, "Oh, Skippee!" Local cuisine in the tropics stressed Paul's Nebraska palate. A whole section in the markets seemed more like shopping in a lumberyard: taro, yams, arrowroot, sugar cane, breadfruit, and other roots and plants that I couldn't identify.

Safety and accident prevention on board become very important for more fragile older bones. Non-skid surfaces may be put on steps; handholds should be placed in appropriate places belowdecks; and loose objects should always be carefully stowed so they don't fly about in rough weather. The larger cruising boats with more amenities also have larger and heavier rigging which, though easily handled with appropriate equipment, may become too heavy in case of disaster or in heavy weather. Procedures for docking, anchoring, and changing sail need to be understood by all, and of course, man-overboard drills should acquaint everyone aboard with his or her responsibilities. On the open seas no one should go on deck without putting on a safety harness and then hooking on, particularly in rough weather.

If the skipper is disabled someone else must run the boat, and for this emergency situation the spouse/friend must know and understand the operation of the navigation systems on the boat, be they GPS, SatNav, Loran, RDF, celestial/coastal, or some combination of these methods. We old-timers know celestial navigation. When satellite navigation systems became

A fruit market in Cádiz, Spain. Left to right, Paul, Emily, Reinhold (crew).

131

available we bought first a SatNav, then a GPS; however, we continue to practice our celestial navigation because we have a natural distrust of the complexity of high-tech gadgets and because electricity at sea is unreliable. You should also be familiar with radar. There should be no mystery to the nautical charts, tide tables, compass, dividers, and parallel rulers. When the course is being plotted you need to be involved in the process—you might have a wise suggestion about the route. If you are going offshore even for a short voyage you may have to stand watches at night and need to know basic navigation. Nevertheless, modern navigational devices are a welcome addition to the offshore cruiser. They do need considerable understanding to use properly, however.

Paul already had a ham radio on board when we set out across the Pacific. He used it daily to communicate with the Pacific net and thus keep in touch with others crossing the ocean at the same time. I could see its value and enjoyment so took a course and got my ham radio operator's license. The VHF radio with which every boat is equipped has a limited range, whereas the ham radio is long range. We found the ham radio to be a useful and valuable resource; we were able to maintain friendships worldwide and had access to valuable information such as the weather and time ticks and help when we needed it. Remember, in spite of your preparation and use of available help, you are on your own if disaster occurs.

Cruising is a perfect time to develop creative interests and hobbies. The ship's library might include books and guides for crafts, crocheting, wood finishing, cooking, bird identification, or whatever you fancy. Nature aficionados like me are in seventh heaven. The creatures we saw in mid-ocean fascinated me. Four shearwaters followed us for many days. When Paul decided to heave-to in order to change the oil, they dropped down and sat on the water, preening and bathing. When we put the sails back up and got under way, they lifted off and continued along with us, swooping and turning gracefully around the boat. Flying fish make a rustling sound as they skitter across the wave tops. We often found dried-out flying fish and squid on the decks in the morning. If the wind died down and the sea was calm we could see any number of small bright fish in the shadow of the boat, possibly seeking shade from the tropic sun or more likely a place to hide. Occasionally we saw the little purple sail of the Portuguese man-o-war traveling alongside. Mahi-mahi are a beautiful fish to watch swimming by your boat; sadly, their rainbow colors fade rapidly when you haul them.

As a long-time Sunday painter I found pen-and-ink sketching very adaptable to the cruising lifestyle, and my sketches are precious mementos of our travels. In order to put an impression down on paper it is necessary to look very carefully at objects or events and understand what is going on. Just a few lines can record a moment in time without all the extraneous stuff a photograph includes.

I am terrified by storms, and we encountered some bad ones. The rolling and thrashing of the boat makes rest impossible and hanging on at all times essential. Calories are needed to provide energy at a time when cooking is most difficult. The stove swings wildly on its gimbals, the pots slide around, the dishes won't stay on the table in spite of fiddles, the food won't stay in the dish, and the meal has been prepared with one hand only. You must take these conditions into account when buying food for the voyage. Trail mix, canned food to be eaten cold (such as fruits or sausages), dry soups, and noodles to be mixed with hot water are some suggestions.

Food planning and preparation are an important part of

cruising. In my opinion cookbooks bought in marine stores seem to be geared to boats with a freezer, refrigerator, stove, oven, and never more than a day or two away from specialty markets. As an exercise you might try preparing a balanced diet with foods bought only at a convenience store plus vegetables that keep without refrigeration. If you venture very far from the United States, this combination may be what you face. Storing vegetables at ambient temperature for six weeks or so requires each potato, onion, green tomato, apple, cabbage, or green banana to be individually wrapped in newspaper. The wrapping protects each item from bruising and isolates any rotten ones from spoiling the entire stores. Some produce keeps better than others do. Carrots keep poorly, and cabbage keeps surprisingly well.

Eggs kept in the egg carton may be stored at room temperature if the carton is turned over every day or two. I understand

Lunch in the cockpit on a sunny day in Greece.

that this has to do with the incubation and hatching of the eggs. Since hens lay only one egg a day, by the end of the incubation period the eggs would hatch one at a time on successive days. No hen can contend with part of her clutch needing to be sat on and the other part now chicks running around. When she first lays the eggs, the hen does not sit on them, but turns them over every day. This keeps the inner membrane moist and prevents spoilage. The eggs then keep until she is ready to incubate them. If we turn the eggs every day or two as the hen does, they stay perfectly fresh (but won't necessarily hatch!).

Banking in foreign countries is now much simpler with electronic transfers of funds and debit cards. You can easily make arrangements for access to your funds prior to departure. A pair of Polish cruisers we met in the South Pacific gave new meaning to the term liquid assets: Faced with a financial dilemma because they were unable to take money out from behind the Iron Curtain, they simply filled their boat with vodka, which they sold along the way for local currency.

Now are you ready to cast off the mooring lines and head for that great adventure?

12

TIPS AND REWARDS

This final chapter is a potpourri of additional tips and suggestions, many of which came from senior cruiser friends to whom I wrote and asked for suggestions. None of these friends are "ancient" in attitude and enthusiasm. Some are in their seventies and still cruising, and some, including me, are in their eighties. So if you are only fifty-five or sixty, imagine the great cruising that you have ahead of you.

TIPS

Shore-based responsibilities. I would suggest that you sell or otherwise dispose of real estate and any other holdings that might require your making a crash visit back home. Because Emily and I were just married when we left the United States, she chose (wisely I presume) to hang on to her house and rent it out while we were gone. This arrangement worked okay for two years. Then Emily concluded that our marriage and the cruising life were compatible and decided to sell her home. We were talking with a tax attorney during a short visit home when he frowned, got out a calendar, and announced, "You have ten days to sell your house or pay about thirty thousand dollars in taxes." We had misinterpreted the applicable tax law. We have heard more than once of other cruisers' quick trips back home to take care of some real-estate problem. Think through your financial affairs and other commitments and make the best arrangements you can before you leave.

The best situation is to have all your wealth in liquid assets such as stocks, bonds, and the like (not mortgages, as you might have to fly home to collect or repossess). Liquid assets can be useful if you need extra cash for unforeseen expenses. Transactions can be handled smoothly with a dependable broker, and you don't have to leave your boat in order to conduct business.

May I also tactfully make a suggestion? Do not leave personal details such as forwarding mail or collecting rents and fees to relatives. In spite of everyone's good intentions, it seldom seems to work out. Like many other cruisers, we contracted with a secretarial service to receive and forward our mail. The fee at that time was modest ($7 a month, plus delivery fees), and our mail was usually on its way the same day we called. Emily had a realtor in charge of renting of her house until it was sold.

Organizations. Belonging to a yacht club brings benefits throughout the world. Many (but not all) yacht clubs give you reciprocal privileges, meaning moorage, perhaps bar and restaurant privileges, and certainly a warm welcome. Carry a few of your burgees and offer to exchange with other clubs, especially if you are made temporary members, as happened to us in New Zealand.

Another organization worth joining is the Seven Seas Cruising Association (SSCA). There are two classes of membership: commodore and associate. Commodores must be living aboard and have completed at least one 2,000-mile, or two 1,000-mile voyages. Associates are anyone else who is cruising or hopes to. SSCA distributes a monthly "Commodore's Bulletin," which publishes letters from members all over the world. We found the bulletin both useful and fun to read. The heavier focus is on piloting and navigational problems, including sketch charts, but the letters also contain wonderful information about local sightseeing, local people, difficulties with customs, and other cautions. The SSCA is both a useful and a proud organization to belong to.

Radio and technological innovations. Not too many years ago the VHF marine radio was the standard way to communicate while in port. Now, cellular phones are proving very useful and workable almost anywhere. (We used ours in Canadian waters last summer to keep in touch with friends on other boats.) There aren't many countries any more that do not have cell phone capability. Cell phones do not, in any sense of the word, replace VHF, single sideband, or ham radio. When satellite phones are more affordable and have global coverage, however, the whole picture will change.

You still need VHF radio because all boats are still required to monitor channel 16 while under way. This requirement isn't just a regulation to be observed under penalty of whatever. It is common sense because you need to communicate with commercial boats and other cruisers in harbor. I was once in an East Coast river, under sail and being chased by a large freighter, when the pilot called and wanted to know my intentions. He stressed that he could not maneuver, and something had to give. I knew, as he did, that there was a sharp bend in the channel ahead. I responded that I was going to hold course, and that in two minutes I would be out of the channel. He thanked me and, I presume, became less nervous about those darn fool skippers who think they have the right of way because they are under sail—they don't.

Another incident illustrates the value of keeping your VHF on channel 16 at all times. We were in U.S. waters on Lake Huron when out of the VHF came a frantic cry, "Mayday! Mayday! My boat is on fire!" The speaker did not answer my requests for his location, nor did he answer the Coast Guard's response. Another sailor radioed that he could see a column of smoke a short distance off his bow. The Coast Guard requested his location, and he responded with his latitude and longitude from his GPS. A commercial vessel then radioed that it was within 3 miles of that point and, with the permission of the Coast Guard, would investigate. Ten minutes later the vessel was at the site of the fire. The skipper was in the water; his boat had burned to the waterline. That sailor is alive today because another sailor and the commercial vessel were monitoring their VHFs on channel 16.

I have great respect for the new electronic navigational systems. However, I would not go offshore without back-up paper charts in my chart drawer. Batteries fail, and searching for a location or feature on a CD in time of stress probably would produce the same kind of confusion and misclicks that my home computer does.

One member of my yacht club who reported to the club regularly commented that their boat had met several cruisers who had e-mail. One worked through the amateur radio, another through a commercial company. This communications link may also be something to check out.

Guns. Whether or not to carry guns on board is a heated subject. I have heard every argument for and against that has been uttered. I carried a knockdown 22 rifle in the South Pacific. At every island that we touched we were required to declare it, check it with the police, and then come back and pick it up when we left. It was a nuisance. However, there are many stories of guns heading off potential confrontations by scaring away locals who appeared unsavory. There are also many stories of guns escalating confrontations to dangerous levels. Two thoughts persist in my mind. First, guns are a nuisance unless you hide them under lock and key and lie about having them aboard—a dangerous gamble that could get you a prison sentence in some countries. Second, I was struck by a comment made by an experienced Vietnam veteran in a debate on this topic published in the house organ of the Seven Seas Cruising Association (of which I am a member). He wrote: "If you are experienced in killing and know your weapon, take it. Unless you can shoot to kill without thinking, you don't need a weapon." Since I can't, I don't.

Apropos guns, there are many areas in the world where piracy prevails still, and there are countries and coasts that do not like Americans or any "rich people with a yacht." We avoided these areas on our voyages. Piracy in the Caribbean still exists somewhat, but there it is not an honorable profession, as it is in some areas of Asia. The drug trade has resulted in some incidents. One SSCA member wrote that his dog was the only protection he needed after it chased off a local who had climbed his anchor chain. The choice is yours; I am neither pro nor con on the subject.

Fresh water. Another member of my yacht club who communicated regularly with the membership reported on problems with the emergency watermaker in their boat's abandon-ship bag. It seemed they had a faulty unit; the factory repaired it,

141

but it failed a second time. We had the same model in our abandon-ship bag, too. Your life may depend on this product; if you get one, please test it *before* you leave.

Potentially malfunctioning equipment is one reason why I still recommend that you carry at least one jerry can of spare water on deck. I know the cans are a nuisance, but they're easy to offload if you have to leave quickly. Just toss them in the water—they will float! I met a couple with two teenage children whose water tank sprang a leak on their passage to the West Coast from Hawaii. The fog was thick, they had two weeks—a thousand miles—to go, and they had no water. They held hands and prayed in the cockpit. Soon the fog cleared, and there was a friendly freighter nearby who had slowed to ask if it could help in any way. That is one way of saving your life,

Lilly, our schipperke guard dog, is third in command of SUNSET, but sometimes assumes greater authority.

142

but a 5-gallon can of fresh water is more dependable. Always be prepared with a tarp to catch rainwater and store it in containers. Use this water to wash your clothes, take a shower, brush your teeth, whatever—and save the fresh water in your tank for drinking.

Standing watch. When you sail offshore, you stand watches. There are many versions of the "best" watch schedule. Emily and I preferred a watch schedule with two hours on and two off. This way we avoided the most dreaded hour of the more standard four on, four off system. For us, that last hour, especially just before dawn, was an eternity. We didn't have posted watches during the day, but someone was always on deck or responsible for putting his or her head out the hatch every ten minutes or so. We took frequent naps during the day and grew lean and healthy under this regimen. But it does need a bit of getting used to. My suggestion is that you play around with different combinations and find what suits you best.

Raising anchor. Because we use all chain rode, we bless the day we had an anchor windlass installed on SUNSET. Ours has two foot controls on deck, one for up and one for down. Other models use hand controls to operate the windlass; there are advantages and disadvantages to both systems. I lean toward the foot controls, because they free your hands to wash the chain as it comes up off the bottom.

There are many ways to rig a seawater pump. SUNSET has a small water pump in the engine room. Many have spoken favorably of attaching a pump to the engine. The advantages of this set-up is that it uses no battery power and you can get a lot of pressure on the hose to really wash down the anchor and the deck. The drawback is that you must have the engine running.

You should run the engine when you both raise and lower the anchor with the windlass. This reduces the heavy current flow since most of your amps are coming from the alternator and not putting too heavy a load on the cable from the anchor battery. In SUNSET, we have a separate battery in the chain locker and also a heavy cable to the starting battery.

Our windlass can also be operated by a hand crank if there is no DC power left on the boat; in my opinion this feature is essential. In case I have difficulty with the hand crank, I also keep a block and tackle on deck. Then, using a chain hook, I can hoist the anchor 3 or 4 feet at a time. Why all this fuss about a 35-pound anchor? Bear in mind that 1 foot of chain weighs approximately 1½ pounds; if you are anchored in 40 feet of water, the chain plus anchor adds up to more than 100 pounds. That is a lot of weight for an old codger to haul up hand over hand.

Handling lines. Whether you have arthritis or not, your grasp is probably not as strong as it once was. Keep a pair of sailing gloves near the hatch so that when you go outside to handle the lines you have a better grip. Another way of improving your grip is to equip the boat with the largest diameter lines that work; figure out a plan with a competent rigger. You may have to replace many of the blocks to accommodate the larger line.

Finally, in the course of outfitting SUNSET we visited a boatyard off Lake Michigan, where we heard about a large sailboat (some 80 feet overall) being built for an eighty-year-old who planned to cruise the Great Lakes and perhaps beyond. It was, according to our informant, completely equipped with hydraulic winches. Talk about easing the strain! I am sure, however, the cost ran to tens of thousands of dollars. If you want power winches, electric winches are a less expensive alternative. You lose a little control but save considerable money. However, there is little need to power every winch; good candidates for not powering are rarely used halyard winches and winches for the smaller sails, such as staysails and the mizzen.

REWARDS

Emily, in the previous chapter, talks about some of the beauties of sea life. Some sights that imprint themselves on your memory are almost beyond belief: Cook's Bay on the French Polynesian island of Moorea, one of the three or four most beautiful spots in the world (in my opinion). And the South Pacific sunsets we observed while watching for the green flash at the precise moment of sundown. Clouds of brightly colored

Vaha's family in Tonga hitched a ride to their nearby island on GOLDEN FLEECE. The young people sang most beautifully along the way.

fish swarming around the reefs. An erupting volcano boiling the water in Tonga (fortunately we were about a mile away). And laughing high school girls strolling the beach in their sarongs after school trying out their English on us. The beautiful islands of New Zealand, hilly and verdant and sprinkled with sheep. The teeming coastal tide pools, which fascinated Emily.

In the Mediterranean we found every island and coast steeped in history. Along with friends who visited us, we began to complain if we didn't get to see at least one ruin each day. I'm talking about such places as Ephesus, the ancient Ionian Greek seaport in modern-day Turkey; about temples to the Greek god Apollo; about watching Shakespeare's *Midsummer Night's Dream* in a 2,000-year-old amphitheater, and seeing camels wrestle in a 2,000-year-old

Our masts now on the deck, we proceed through Chicago during the morning rush hour.

athletic field while nearby Turks cook their lunch over small fires. In France, we drifted at 5 knots down canals across farmland, across bridges (yes, across), and under the multitude of beautiful Paris bridges. Preparing for the Atlantic crossing at Gibraltar, we experienced a microcosm of British culture surrounded by Mediterranean Spain and Morocco. Watching a polo match on Cyprus, we shared a bottle of wine with a nearly toothless Greek owner of a restaurant on one of the smaller islands, chattering and laughing for fifteen minutes and having a wonderful time; he spoke no English, and we spoke no Greek.

On the East Coast of the United States, the images are no less spectacular: Dodging a nuclear submarine in a river channel, attending (in our dinghy with friends) the graduation ceremony of the U.S. Naval Academy at Annapolis while the Blue Angels performed their intricate maneuvers overhead. The absolute awesome thrill of watching the space shuttle *Columbia* take off from Cape Canaveral while having coffee on our afterdeck. Seeing the New York City skyline and the Statue of Liberty from the deck of our own boat. In the Midwest, we were slowly cruising past the giant skyscrapers of Chicago while on either side the poor natives, carrying their briefcases, hurried to their jobs.

Every minute of these adventures was experienced on the deck of our home or close by or within hiking or cycling distance. We needed no reservations and no tour guides, and we could stay as long as we liked. We prepared most of our own meals, but occasionally the cook had a night out on the town. If this sounds like an ideal existence it was—almost! You pay your dues with fewer conveniences than you find in a house and some moments of fright when things go bump in the night. And, now that we are ashore, Emily finally has some ground for her second, or third, or something, love, which is gardening. I have time to write, and we ski and spend time on our boat in safe waters. Nobody except another cruiser can appreciate the glorious memories that we have.

Appendix

SELECTED REFERENCES

There are several books that ought to be read by everyone who plans to put to sea. While there is no substitute for experience, there is also no substitute for preparation. The latter tends to prevent unhappy experiences from happening and creates a good climate for happy ones. In addition to references mentioned in individual chapters, the books described below are among those that I have appreciated for their completeness and usefulness.

Survivor, by Michael Greenwald
Survivor covers almost every serious accident that could happen at sea, including sinking and being castaway. We met Greenwald in the South Pacific and also Gary Mundell, whose fifty-five days on Caroline Island is one of the survival stories Greenwald analyzes. The book covers the prevention of accidents in incredible detail, but in my opinion, its chief value is found in Greenwald's conclusion that survivors are those who have a strong will to survive.

Self-Steering Without a Wind Vane, by Lee Woas
This work describes almost every way that a sailboat can be made to steer itself. Reading it helps you understand your boat better, and you may be thankful you included it in the ship's library if your wind vane breaks. I referred to it in the Tuamotus, French Polynesia when ours lost a rudder; its advice got us to Tahiti.

Emergency Navigation, by David Burch
This book's subtitle, *Pathfinding Techniques for the Inquisitive and Prudent Mariner*, is a good description of its value. You can learn much about the sea and stars reading this volume— and then hope you never need to use this knowledge.

We, The Navigators, by David Lewis
This is a story of the last of the great Polynesian navigators. Dr. Lewis befriended him and wrote this book to preserve his knowledge. A resurgence of interest in traditional Polynesian methods of navigation followed, as have other books. This is a delightful, informative volume.

Understanding Rigs and Rigging, by Richard Henderson
Henderson's work is a complete and updated discussion of the subject. Recent changes in rig designs and materials may affect your boat-buying decisions.

Royce's Sailing Illustrated, by Patrick M. Royce
This handy little book, which has been through many editions, will amaze you with its completeness. I have owned one since it was first published in 1956. It is really all about sailing, but I value it most for its illustrations of the various rigs of tall ships. If you are, or plan to be, a sailor, you need it aboard.

Selected References

Anchoring, by Brian M. Fagan
While many how-to books include a chapter on anchoring and model-specific information is available free from many manufacturers, this work is quite complete and well illustrated. You need to know several ways to anchor and especially how to clear a fouled anchor.

World Cruising Routes, by Jimmy Cornell
The author draws from official publications, other world cruisers, and his own experiences to recommend routes to be traveled by small boats. This information is organized into easily understood segments by region. For example, a section of the ocean is shown crossed with numbered routes. For each route, the text that follows describes weather and current patterns, relevant charts and publications, and other navigational concerns, all from the point of view of small boats, not of commercial vessels, as is the case in most government publications. This book is useful for planning a world cruise.

The Self-Sufficient Sailor, by Larry and Lin Pardey
Larry is a somewhat controversial sailing purist and has every right to be so. One of his statements in this book is "If you can't fix it, you shouldn't have it aboard." For example, on the Pardey boats, there have been no motors and all fluid systems have been fed by gravity or hand pumps. You will learn a lot from this book about boats and how to simplify your life aboard.

Cruising French Waterways, by Hugh McKnight
Cruising French Waterways is a marvelous descriptive guide to the astonishingly varied network of rivers and canals that

penetrate almost every region of France. It is full of fascinating information on the historical sites, chateaux and scenic attractions of the many villages and towns which await discovery by water.

National Audubon Society Field Guide to North American Weather, by David M. Ludlum
This absolutely fascinating book provides descriptions and explanations of every weather phenomenon. The center section contains a fantastic series of brilliant photographs of clouds and other weather conditions. If you really want to study weather, you can use this book.

We have also enjoyed reading about others' experiences cruising. Frequently these books contain descriptions of or suggestions for rigging, comfort, safety, housekeeping, and other items that have worked well for us aboard our boats. Here are some with which I am familiar.

All in the Same Boat, by Fiona McCall and Paul Howard

Mahina Tiare: Pacific Passages, by Barbara Marrett and John Neal

Gentlemen Never Sail to Weather, by Denton Rickey Moore

Cruising in SERAFFYN, by Lin and Larry Pardey

You'll find many, many more cruising adventures to intrigue you at your bookstore or library and available through the catalogues of the nautical book publishers Sheridan House and International Marine. Of course, we hope you'll also want

Selected References

to read more about our own adventures in *Sailing the Golden Sea* and *Sailing the Inland Seas*, both by Paul H. Keller and published by Portside Publishing, Portland, Oregon. Good reading!

INDEX

INDEX

Index

INDEX

hypertension, 114–15, 118–19
hypoglycemia, 104, 105

illness, 102–5, 114–26
immigration, 12–15
immunizations, 12–15
injuries, 101–11
   head, 110
   intra-abdominal, 110–11
International Radio Medical
   Center, 101
inverters, 87–89, 90
Ishihara, Ruth, 94

keel, 25, 27–28
kidney stones, 124–25

language, 12–15
laptop, 65, 75
Lee, E. C. B., 101
Lee, Kenneth, 101
leukocytes, 123
Lewis, David, 68, 150
lifelines, 48–49, 51
liferaft, 54, 55
Lifesling, 54
lighting, 27, 42, 44
lights, white, 67
line handling, 144–45
liveaboards, 7, 8
Living on Twelve Volts with
   Ample Power
   (Smead and Ishihara),
   94
London, Jack, 5
Ludlum, David M., 152
lung problems, 117, 119–20

Mahina Tiare: Pacific Passages
   (Marrett and Neal),
   152
Mail, 138
main saloon, 43
Maloney, Elbert S., 59
man overboard, 53–56, 130
Mariners Met Pack, South
   Pacific (McDavitt), 75
Marrett, Barbara, 152
masts, 24, 25, 56–58
McCall, Fiona, 152
McDavitt, Bob, 75
McKnight, Hugh, 151–52
medical kit, 99–101
medications, 99–100, 103–13,
   115–26, 128
mental acuity, 113
mental attitude, ix–x, 6
Mitchell, Harry and Marge,
   71–72
money, 12–15, 135
Moore, Denton Rickey, 152
Mundell, Gary, 149

National Audubon Society Field
   Guide to North
   American Weather
   (Ludlum), 152
navigation
   celestial, 66, 68, 131–32
   electronic, 64–65, 140
   emergency, 130–32, 150
   station, 42–43
Neal, John, 152
neurological problems, 125–26
   transient ischemic attack
   (TIA), 125

Index

nitroglycerin, 99, 117, 118
numbness, 126

organizations, 138–39
osteoporosis, 101–2, 109, 128
outboard motor, 82–83

padeye, 51–52
Paine, Chuck, 86
Pardey, Larry, 5, 9, 57, 151, 152
Pardey, Lin, 5, 9, 151, 152
part-timers, 6–7
pericarditis, 117
peripheral neuropathy, 126
piloting, 59–68
piracy, 141
pneumonia, 120
portholes, 25–26
prostate, 99, 123

radar, 61, 67–68, 132
radio, 100–101
    innovations, 139–40
rainwater, 143
real estate, 137–38
reflexes, 102
refrigeration, 41–42, 88
resistance heating, 88
responsibilities, shore-based, 137–38
rewards, 145–48
rigging, 28, 31, 32–37, 51, 130
righting moment, 27
roller furling, 33–35
Royce, Patrick M., 150
Royce's Sailing Illustrated (Royce), 150

rudder, 27
rust, 24

safety, 47–58, 130
    abandon-ship routine, 55–56
    abovedecks, 48–53
    aloft, 56–58
    belowdecks, 48
    handy-billy, 53, 54
    harness, 11, 49, 51–52, 57, 130
    in the water, 53–56
Safety and Survival at Sea (Lee and Lee), 101
Sail, 15
sailing skills, 5, 15–17
Sailing the Golden Sea, 3, 153
Sailing the Inland Seas, 3, 153
sailplans, 30–31
sails, 30–32, 37
seasickness, 16–17, 113
Seven Seas Cruising Association (SSCA), 138–39, 141
seizure, 102–3, 125–26
Self-Sufficient Sailor, The (Pardey and Pardey), 151
Self-Steering Without a Wind Vane (Woas), 150
sensory problems, 112–13
sextant, 66
sight, 98, 112–13
sightseeing, 11–12, 132–33, 145–48
single-sideband radio system (SSB), 75
skeg, 27
skin cancer, 114

The Mariner's Library Fiction Classics Series

BALTIC MISSION
A NATHANIEL DRINKWATER NOVEL
by Richard Woodman

Captain Nathaniel Drinkwater and his frigate HMS ANTIGONE are ordered to the Baltic on an urgent and delicate mission. As Napoleon's forces push on towards Russia, Drinkwater faces his oldest enemy and is pushed to the brink of death.

IN DISTANT WATERS
A NATHANIEL DRINKWATER NOVEL
by Richard Woodman

Captain Nathaniel Drinkwater confronts formidable enemies, mutiny and a beautiful and mysterious ally. Off the coast of San Francisco, he is struck with an extraordinary twist of fate.

A PRIVATE REVENGE
A NATHANIEL DRINKWATER NOVEL
by Richard Woodman

Assigned to escort a mysterious convoy with a single passenger along the China coast, Captain Drinkwater is drawn into a vicious web of treachery, perversity and greed, culminating in a climactic rendezvous in the remote tropical rainforests of Borneo.

UNDER FALSE COLOURS
A NATHANIEL DRINKWATER NOVEL
by Richard Woodman

Acting for the Admiralty's Secret Department in the dregs of London's docklands, Captain Nathaniel Drinkwater advertises his cargo of Russian military supplies, thus embarking on a scheme to flout Napoleon's Continental System and antagonize the French Emperor's new ally, Tsar Alexander.

THE FLYING SQUADRON
A NATHANIEL DRINKWATER NOVEL
by Richard Woodman

Amid the internationally acrimonious atmosphere of 1811, Captain Nathaniel Drinkwater stumbles upon a bold conspiracy by which the U.S. could defeat the Royal Navy, collapse the British government and utterly destroy the British cause.

America's Favorite Sailing Books
www.sheridanhouse.com